Dubbed Britain's foremost authority on curries and spicy food, Pat Chapman is best known for his many cookery books, which have sold around one million copies worldwide. In 1982 Pat founded *The Curry Club*, which has 15,000 members. He is a frequent radio and television broadcaster.

Pat Chapman's
THAI
RESTAURANT
COOKBOOK

Hodder & Stoughton

Acknowledgements

The props and dishes in these photographs were purchased in Bangkok's markets and shops. We are grateful to the staff of the Oriental Hotel, Bangkok, for their assistance, and especially to London's Blue Elephant Thai Restaurant for donating all the fruit and vegetable carvings.

Photography by Colin Poole.

Food for photography prepared and styled by Pat and Dominique Chapman.

First published in Great Britain in 1996 by Hodder and Stoughton.
A division of Hodder Headline PLC.
First published in paperback in 1997.

A CIP catalogue record of this book is available from the British Library.

ISBN 0 340 68036 9

Printed and bound in Great Britain by Mackays of Chatham PLC

Hodder and Stoughton
A division of Hodder Headline PLC
338 Euston Road
London NW1 3BH

CONTENTS

FOREWORD

'I GUESS YOU either love Thai food or you don't,' I was told by a US General years ago. He'd found out that I'd been brought up on spicy curries. 'It's not like Indian food at all,' he cautioned me. 'But it is spicy and herby, sweet and sour, fragrant and hot. Done right it should be subtle. I guess you'll love it.'

I guessed I would, but my problem was I'd never tasted it, and there were no Thai restaurants in Britain then. There were precious few Indian or Chinese restaurants, for that matter either.

The year was 1964, the location the west of England. I'd not long since joined the RAF and was stationed at South Cerney, Gloucestershire. One day, a group of us were enjoying the pleasures of our nearby 'local', when in came some young USAF aircrew from their base at nearby Fairford. Soon, in a scene full of clichés from wartime movies, we were contesting each other to yards of ale. I don't recall who won, but the outcome was a return challenge at their base.

I remember being momentarily shocked by the raucous atmosphere of their officers' club. It was like a Dallas bar, awash with stetson wearers, the noisiest of whom, a John Wayne look-alike, was playing bucking bronco, complete with lasso and jingling spurs. His mount, the wildest of steers, was a bar stool! The entire bar was yelping encouragement. We were amazed to find out that 'John Wayne' was not only the station commander, he was a veteran one-star general, that same general I mentioned above.

'Make yourself at home,' he yelled .'I guess this ain't a bit like your mess.'

'No Sir,' we agreed, wondering if he'd ever been to an RAF Dining-In-Night, when its normally hushed and cloistered respectability turns into a bedlam of mess games.

We were struck speechless when we found out that we had to pay for our drinks in US dollars, not a currency easily obtained at the time in Gloucestershire. When 'John Wayne' got to hear of our dilemma, he solved it with typical American generosity: 'It's on the house for the Limeys,' he bellowed.

Our new-found USAF friends told us they were just about to be posted for a year to Vietnam. This was the time when President Johnson was escalating that war. They had plenty to say about Johnson and the war, none of it good. All they looked forward to were their leave periods, which they would spend in Thailand.

As the Budweisers flowed we all waxed lyrical about leave, aeroplanes, beer and Bangkok. We knew a bit about the first three, but nothing about the latter. 'John Wayne' joined us, telling us he'd been based there. It was then that he told us about the delights of Thai food. He was so persuasive that we all agreed it was one of the most visitable places on earth. There and then, I resolved to visit the country.

The opportunity came ten years later. My work took me to Hong Kong and thence to New Zealand for a busy month. I elected to travel on the once mighty Pan Am airline, whose round-the-world flight departed daily in each direction out of New York. The east-bound flight first stopped in London, where I boarded it, then flew on to Frankfurt, Rome, Beirut, Bahrein, Delhi, Bangkok, and Hong Kong. Even though the aircraft was a Boeing 747, the flight to Hong Kong, with all those stops, took over 30 hours. There were quicker alternatives, but Pan Am 001 had one irresistible advantage for me – Bangkok.

Since I had a couple of days to spare, what better place to spend the time? I was allocated a window seat in the rear-most row. Storms over Europe, then early dark, meant there was nothing to see enroute, and I quickly got bored with transit lounges. Dawn came in India. One of the most memorable sights of my life was the early morning sun glinting on the Himalayas, miles to the north, as we flew from Delhi to Bangkok.

I reviewed what I knew about Thailand. It wasn't much. I'd never eaten Thai food. Nor had my midwife mother, who'd had a thing about Siamese twins. I thought Siamese cats were the world's prettiest pets. I'd seen *The King and I* and *The Bridge on the River Kwai*. That was about it. I thought a lot about those lads from Fairford, a decade previously.

Two days later, Bangkok visited for the first time, they were uppermost in my mind when I resumed my window vantage point aboard another plane, this time heading for Hong Kong. Shortly after take-off I saw two USAF Phantom jets slide into formation behind and below us. They stayed with us for about half an hour, until we were over the South China Sea. During much of that time we were overflying South Vietnam. This was at the climax of the Vietnam War. Even more unforgettable were the countless bomb craters, many filled with water, glinting like vast circular lakes. I wondered what had become of my American friends. But what of their advice? Was it all true?

Bangkok in the early 1970s was astoundingly different to today's mega-city as we approach the year 2000. I remember a smaller Bangkok in 1973 with a skyline more of trees, pagodas, palaces and temples, than of tower-blocks, though building was underway apace. The air was scented with flowers, and the mighty river Chao Praya was clean and quiet. From it sprouted canals in every direction, upon which gondolas were paddled by people in national dress and bamboo hats. There were fewer people then and the roads were quiet and unpolluted. Cycle rickshaws still dominated. The shops traded modestly out of old teak buildings.

I had found Thailand, the land of the free. To this day it remains a colourful, joyous place with many fairy-tale ingredients. Royals, palaces, golden temples, elephants, endless fertile farms and exquisite countryside are some which spring to mind. It has a people with a noble history, a gracious culture, exotic costume, serene swaying dance, a soft sing-song language, and dulcet gentle music from wooden xylophones. They are outstandingly beautiful people, seemingly always smiling, the men as delectable as the women. They always appear unruffled and their phrase *mai pen rai* (never mind) is never far from their lips. Neither are their two concepts of *sabai* (serenity) and *sanuk* (fun).

And what of Thai food? On that first visit, I don't recall eating at my hotel. I discovered the delights of Bangkok's street vendors. Then, as now, they plied their culinary wares at every opportunity (*see page 15*). My two days flashed by in a whirl of grazing from trader to trader, from morning to night. My travels had already taken me to many an outflung destination, but I'd never come across anything as varied as this. And the beauty of street hawkers, for one who collects recipes, is that you can see exactly how the item you are about to eat is made. So began my passion for Thai food.

It was to take a few more years before the first Thai restaurants opened in Britain. Without exception, they set a standard for Thai cuisine which was top-notch. The British public, predictably, have welcomed Thai cuisine with open arms.

In the last three years the number of Thai restaurants has nearly doubled to some 500 establishments up and down the country. However, even though this represents only a three per cent share of the total British ethnic restaurant market, an expansion of this volume is fraught with danger. Lack of sufficiently well trained cooks can result in the new restaurants presenting a mere caricature of the very food they are trying to present. It is all too easy to slip into a formula. It is the same at Indian and Chinese restaurants, of which by now there are thousands. Many operate to a formula, the net result of which is to give its cuisine a poor reputation. This is one reason why curry, for example, has earned itself a down-market image, which no amount of top-notch new Indian restaurants have yet dispelled.

At worst, the Thai formula relies too heavily on Chinese cuisine, made 'Thai' by injudicious use of chilli, sugar and coconut milk. And this is not because of a lack of Thai ingredients. Neither is it cost driven. It is simply a lack of culinary talent in the kitchen.

Fortunately, since the Thai restaurant is still in its honeymoon period, the media on the whole treat Thai food with respect – according it a position almost as up-market as French.

Fay Maschler, one of Britain's most respected restaurant critics, described this as 'wonderment' in a review in London's *Evening Standard*, dated 3 March 1996. She described the formula cuisine as presented in certain Thai restaurants as of 'monotonous quality'. She went on: 'Deep-frying as a cooking method, sugar as a flavouring and chilli as a kick are instantly appealing, but it is the appeal of much fast food…and has the clinging aura of children's food.'

I hasten to repeat that this is not the case with all Thai restaurants. Indeed, Miss Maschler took pains to point out that the particular restaurant she was reviewing (the Nipa Thai at the Royal Lancaster Hotel), transcended this trap ('apart from predictably banal set menu round-ups') and she praised its food for its balance of flavour and texture sensations. The Nipa is not the only Thai restaurant with the ability to produce Thai food correctly. Amongst others, London's Blue Elephant remains my favourite, with the Khun Akorn, and the Chiang Mai close behind.

The Thai restaurant boom is set to continue growing at a rapid rate. Whether its product will remain in the ascendant is in the restaurateur's hands. But the restaurants must be diligent if they wish to retain their position of respect. At Indo-Bangladeshi restaurants, British diners have become considerably more expert and discerning than they were in the early 1980s. Soon this will be the case in Thai restaurants.

I hope this book will help. It is from the top-notch restaurants, including those in Thailand, and not forgetting those DIY street hawkers, that I have assembled this collection of favourite Thai recipes. I sincerely hope you try them all. I hope this book will introduce Thai food fans to new dishes as well as reacquainting them with their old favourites.

The ability to cook at home never diminishes trade at the better restaurants. If anything, it increases it, with the diner-cook the more able to tell the good from the bad. I adore cooking, as I expect you do, too. But there are times when I simply do not want to be bothered. Going to the restaurant on such an occasion is so much more alluring and fun. But I also love the challenge of being able to do it at home.

Here, with the time to create it in the way you want it to be, and with this book at your side, you'll find that cooking Thai food is relatively quick, the results completely rewarding, the variety amazing, the tastes subtle, and the textures superb. I'm sure you won't just like it, you'll love it.

That US General guessed right all those years ago. I expect he's still enjoying himself. I wonder if he remembers some callow English youths with no dollars.

Pat Chapman
Haslemere
July 1996

MENUS

Like most others, Thais eat three meals a day: breakfast, lunch and dinner. And like for most of us, the average home meal is straightforward, as represented in the first three example menus below. Do please remember these are just examples. They give the way a Thai meal is structured (*see also Page 25*). You can make your own substitutes or additional dishes.

Again, like us, Thais do enjoy their more elaborate meals when entertaining or celebrating. The final three examples take care of those occasions.

Thais are great grazers. In the cities, hawkers and market cafés make food available on a twenty-four-hour basis. For a quick any-time graze, make any soup or salad, or perhaps a noodle dish, from Chapters 3, 4 and 11.

I've given two more menu examples – one vegetarian and the other for the different picnic.

To any of these examples you should add as many chutneys, sauces and pickles from Chapter 12 as take your fancy. The suggested number of servings is given for each recipe, but you can adjust quantities pro rata as required.

BREAKFAST OR BRUNCH

SERVES: 1 OR MORE

Khao Tom Kai (breakfast rice) *page 75*
Yam Naw Mia Farang (asparagus salad) *page 85*
Khao Taang (sweet rice crispy chips) *page 70*
Lemon Grass Tea *page 189*

LIGHT LUNCH OR TV SUPPER

SERVES: 4

Kai Jeow (omelette) *page 108*
and/or
Pad Thai (stir-fried noodles) *page 158*
or
Khai Khaeng (curry over rice). Any curry from Chapter 9 and
rice from Chapter 10.

A TYPICAL THAI MEAL

SERVES: 4

Si-Khrong Moo Tod (ribs) *page 93*
Tom Yam Nua (beef soup) *page 73*
Yam Talai (seafood salad) *page 83*
Khaeng Ked-Wan Gai (green curry with chicken) *page 140*
Khao Pad Horapa (basil fried rice) *page 155*

I-sa Gereem Katee (coconut ice cream) *page 188*
Polamai (fresh fruit) *page 181*

A THAI PICNIC

A selection of cold dishes for a hot day in the open air.

SERVES: 4 TO 6

Satay Moo (chicken satay) *page 59*
Kari Pub (curry puffs) *page 60*
Kanom Pang Grawp (crackers) *page 70*
Pla Nua Yaang Gub Aa-ngoon (salad of stir-fried beef with
grapes) *page 80*
Look Cheen Ping (meat balls on skewers) *page 90*
Khao Yam (rice salad) *page 156*

A THAI VEGETARIAN MEAL

————— SERVES: 4 TO 6 —————

Serve all together or as three or four courses.
Pak Tod (vegetable fritters) *page 68*

*

Pak Gaeng-Chud (vegetable consommé) *page 76*

*

Yam Phonlamai (savoury fruit salad) *page 87*
Nam Prig Ong (northern chilli vegetable) *page 126*
Galumbi Har Tao Hou (spicy mushroom with tofu) *page 127*
Khao Pad Maprao (coconut rice) *page 155*

*

Kruay Chueam (caramelized sweet bananas) *page 184*

THAI RESTAURANT FAVOURITE FOUR COURSE DINNER

————— SERVES: 4 TO 6 —————

This menu will require planning and advance work (see note on page XVI).
Kanom Pang Grawp (crackers) *page 70*
Satay Gai (chicken satay) *page 59*
Por Pia Tod (prawn spring roll) *page 62*
Kanom-Pang Moo Gung (prawn toast) *page 69*

*

Tom Yam Gai (chicken soup) *page 73*
Yam Yai ('Large' vegetable salad) *page 85*

*

Talai Thai (seafood special) *page 117*
Khaeng Panaeng Nua (Malay-style beef curry) *page 145*
Khao Pad Kai (egg fried rice) *page 155*

*

Kruay Tod (bananas fritters) *page 185*

A GOURMET FOUR COURSE DINNER

Inspired by Bangkok's Shangri-La and Oriental Hotels, this meal comprises some of the lesser known treasures from Thailand.

As with the previous menu, and the Royal Feast which follows, you will need to plan the making of this menu. See note overleaf.

———————————— SERVES: 4 TO 6 ————————————

Bai Kruay Too-ay (filled banana leaf cup) *page 52*
Krathak (pastry cloaked prawn) *page 64*

*

Ped Gaeng-Chud Manao Dong (duck consommé with
vinegared lime) *page 77*

*

Yam Kuaytiaw Sen Mee (noodle salad with mango and orange)
page 162
Nua-Look-Gaa Pad Bai-salanai (lamb stir-fried with mint)
page 97
Pla Nang Moo Issan (pork salad) *page 82*
Khaeng Leung Pa-Moo Yaang (yellow curry with wild boar)
page 143
Khao Niaw Daeng (black rice) *page 152*

*

Fug Thawng Sang-Khaya (pumpkin custard) *page 187*

A RIGHT ROYAL FEAST

For a particularly festive occasion.

SERVES: 8 TO 10 (FIVE COURSES)

From the Thai royal repertoire, this collection of recipes will require careful planning and some advance work using freezer and fridge. The starters, though needing the deep-fryer on the day could, for example, come from the freezer, as can the soup, liver and curry. The pudding and the rice can be put in the fridge the day before. The salad and asparagus must be made as freshly as possible. Because there are so many dishes, the recipes will provide sufficient for 8 to 10 people, except desserts. If you think you have big appetites, the rice and soup could be doubled.

Moo Sarong (golden thread pork) *page 55*
Gai Har Bai Toey (emerald parcels) *page 56*
Tung Tong (fried filled golden bags) *page 66*
*
Tom Yam Talai (seafood soup) *page 72*
*
Yam Gai Tua-Pu (chicken and winged-bean salad) *page 84*
*
Tab Gai Pad Prig (spicy chicken liver) *page 104*
Doon Naw-Mai-Farang (steamed asparagus) *page 129*
Bai Horapa Tord Grob (crisp fried basil leaves) *page 133*
Khaeng Myanmar Ped (Burmese-style duck curry) *page 146*
Khao Pa-Som (black and white rice) *page 152*
Mee Grob (crispy noodles) *page 164*
*
Khao Tom Mat Som (rubies with orange segments) *page 186*

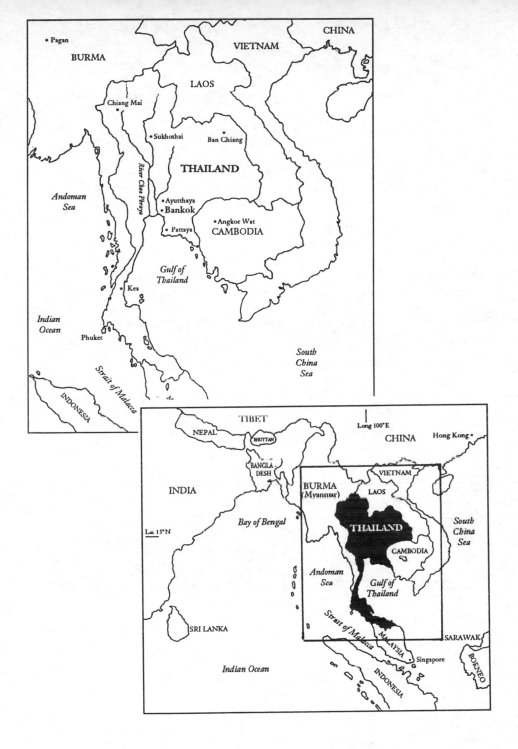

XVII

INTRODUCTION

THAILAND HAS the distinction of being the most stable country in Indo-China, with, as we shall see, a continuous rule by a succession of Thai kings from the twelfth century to this day. For much of this time it was known as Siam, and although it was never occupied by China or India, its food and its people were greatly influenced by both mighty nations. Since its borders expanded to encompass Cambodia, Laos, Vietnam, Malaya and Burma on more than one occasion, it is not surprising that these influences played their important part too, especially in culinary terms. Thailand's food, however, developed along a course of its own, summarizing a nation, which, far from being colonized by a European 'master', managed to banish them from its shores, at the most crucial point in its development.

When the West finally discovered Thai food, as late as the 1960s, we quickly realized what we had been missing. Thai restaurants exploded into our culture, first in the USA, then Australia, and, latterly, only in the last fifteen years, in Britain. What we had been missing was neither Indian nor Chinese. It was unique.

True, there are curries, but they are quite different from their Indian cousins. True, there are noodle dishes, and spring rolls and wontons, but their flavourings and fillings are Thai, not Chinese. Rice dishes are the staple, true, but where else can you get jasmine fragranced rice?

And if one had to use just one word to differentiate Thai food from everyone else's, the word I'd use is 'fragrance'. In Thai cuisine, fragrance comes from a remarkable balance of ingredients, especially fresh herbs, notably basil and coriander. Further fragrance comes from lemon grass and kaffir lime leaves. In common with many races in Asia, Thais love chillies, some of which are really hot, whilst they use hardly any spices. Sour tastes appear now and again in the form of tamarind and kaffir lime. Savoury tastes come from garlic, onion, and ginger in the form of the indigenous galangal. A hint of fudge-like palm sugar is countered with equally subtle hints of salty fish sauce and shrimp paste, but never in sufficient quantities to enable the diner to identify any one of them. Meat, poultry, fish and shellfish, being relatively expensive and scarce resources in Thailand, appear in modest quantities in their cooking, combined usually with a wide range of vegetables, lightly cooked to retain their crunchy goodness.

It is these ingredients, now becoming widely available in the West, which correctly combined, make Thai food unique. Cooking techniques range from stir-frying to steaming, and deep-frying to boiling. Textures range from the crunchiest items to the softest. Hot and cold dishes are served alongside each other.

Any culinary style is made distinctive by what ingredients are *not* used. In Thai cooking, as in Chinese, dairy products are absent. Milk, cream, yoghurt, butter and cheese play no part. In this respect, Thai cooking could not be more different from Indian. Bread, and most wheat products, are absent too. And the absence of oven cooking could give Thai food limitations. In the West, we are convinced we cannot do without all these ingredients, yet when we enjoy a Thai meal, we are unaware that they are, in fact, not there. Such is the strength of Thai food.

In this book I have chosen the widest range of Thai favourites that I can. You should find all the favourites of the western Thai restaurant menu. But in addition, I have included dishes which are less familiar. But I can say that I have met each and every one of them, either on Thailand's streets, courtesy of her fabulous food vendors, or from her restaurants, up and down the country.

I'm looking forward to introducing you to all of them, but before we get busy in the kitchen, I'd like you to join me on a journey to Thailand to find out where she is, to meet her people, and to see how her nation, food and restaurants here evolved over the centuries to become so special and unique.

WHERE IS THAILAND?

CENTRED AT 15°N latitude and 100°E longitude, Thailand is a tropical country bordering Indo-China, extending north to south some 1600km in length, and at its widest 1000km east to west. The shape of its 514,000 sq km land mass (which is over twice that of the UK) is very aptly described by its inhabitants as that of an elephant's head, since the elephant is the national animal, and is very highly revered

Most of that land mass forms the elephant's head. The mountain range in the north and north-west forms not only the 'skull' but a natural border with Burma. The point where the borders with Burma, Laos and Thailand meet is delineated by the conjoining of the rivers Mekong and Ruak. This area of outstanding beauty is known as 'The Golden Triangle'. Laos forms the 'ears' and Cambodia the 'jaw'. The 1000km long thin isthmus is the trunk stretching southwards until it joins the Malaysia penninsula.

THAILAND'S PEOPLE

THAILAND'S POPULATION is around 60 million, of which the majority (45 million) are Thai, of several ethnic groups with dialectic differences. There are 6.5 million Chinese Thais. Of the two million Malay Thais, most are Moslem.

The remainder of the population are descendants of the Mons (Burmese), Khmer (Cambodia), Laotian and Vietnamese. The hill tribes of Thailand's far north account for well under one million people. They are nomadic and borderless and wear beautiful and distinctive costumes.

Ninety per cent of the population are Buddhists. The country has 27,000 temples and every Buddhist male must serve time as a monk.

Seventy per cent of the population work on the land, living in villages of between 100 and 150 houses, typically built on wooden poles or stilts above or alongside canals (*klongs*), in extended families of between four and ten people. Between them they fish, or farm chickens, ducks or water-buffalo. They harvest 20 million tons of rice per annum.

PRONOUNCING THE THAI LANGUAGE

I HAVE GIVEN the Thai names for all the recipes in this book and for many ingredients in the glossary. This is to help your ordering at the Thai restaurant or grocery store. To those not familiar with the Thai language, it looks strange and incomprehensible. Though it developed from Chinese centuries ago, it is not as guttural. It flows easier, and is distinguishable by the rather beautiful sing-song intonations. This is the result of being economical with words. I mean by this that one word can have a number of meanings, depending on which of five tones are applied to it. These are high, middle or low voice pitches, and a rising or lowering of intonation. To make it more complex, some Thai words look similar. For example *ped* is duck. And *pad pak paad ped pa phet* means 'stir-fried vegetables with spicy minced wild duck'.

Whereas English has 21 consonants, Thai has some 40. The extras are soft or aspirated sounds.

For example, 'T' can be pronounced hard (staccato) or less hard when it becomes almost 'Th' (although it is still lighter than the English th as in the). D can also have as many variations. When it comes to translating Thai phonetics to English, there are therefore several ways of attempting to spell any one word.

Take *Tom* (boil). It can also appear as *Thom, thhom, dhom* or *dom*. The Thai word for prawn can vary from *kung* to *ghoong*. Thai vowels are equally complex and generally dipthonged, or composite in sound. The English word 'ate', is an example, traversing from 'a' to 'ee'. The Thai word *Khaeng* (meaning curry liquid) is an example. Pronounced soft 'k' - ar-yen-g, it can also be spelt *kaeng kaing, kaueng* or *gaeng* and look how similar it is to *kung* or *ghoong* above. Of course to a Thai (ignoring dialects) there is only one way to pronounce each word.

It is only the phonetic translations from Thai to English and back again which create difficulties.

This explains why no two Thai travel or cookbooks, or restaurant menus, written in English agree on spelling. Take the word 'noodle'. A flip through ten books produces the following variations (in alphabetical order) *guautiaw, gueyteow, gwaytio, kuaytiaw, kwaytiew, kwaytio* and *kwitiaw*.

In this book I have chosen one spelling method, and have applied it consistently to every word. My preferred version of noodles for example, is *kuaytiaw*. Where a consonant is pronounced softly I have added an 'h' to the word. For example *kuaytiaw* has a more or less hard 'k' (though slightly softer than our word king). *Khaeng* (curry sauce) is very soft, which I have indicated with the addition of the 'h' after the 'k'. All these problems occur in translating written Thai to English.

Thais also have problems with spoken English. Some words are tongue twisters. They cannot pronounce a trilled 'r' by rolling the tongue and a word such as green curry would be pronounced 'gerleen khaee'. 'Th' is difficult and 's' adjacent to 'p' and 't' causes problems. So a 'three gram teaspoon' would be pronounced 'terlee gerlam tee serpoon'. The inability to say the word 'steak' is said to have led to the invention of the word *satay*, 'stew' becomes *satu*, and 'ice cream', *isa gereem.*

Since I cannot string two Thai words together, my comments may appear derisory. I assure you they are not. Thai language is beautiful, the limitations, only when speaking English, charming.

I can't resist telling you about one tongue twisting anecdote. Dominique and I had been shopping in the Bangkok markets. We went for lunch in a posh restaurant, and put our carrier bags on the floor next to my chair. A waiter came along to take our order, tripped over our bags, and landed virtually on top of me. 'Kiss me'. he said. It took us a few seconds to realise he meant 'Excuse me', but found the combination of 'exc' impossible to say! It gives a whole new meaning to Admiral Lord Nelson's last words!

THAILAND'S HISTORY

AS HAS BEEN mentioned, the two great influences on Thai food are Chinese and Indian. From early times, Indian and Chinese mariners had connected their two vast countries in a trade route which compelled them to pass through the narrow Straits of Malacca. There they had to wait for a change of monsoon wind direction before they could proceed. Archaeologists know that iron tools, probably from China, were in use in Thailand as early as 500 BC, and it is around this period that Chinese and Indian mariners began to trade here. More significantly, the Indians brought their religions. Dr KT Achaya, in his book, *Indian Food, an Historical Companion* (OUP, Bombay), says: *'Hindu and Buddhist kingdoms could hardly have been established all over south-east Asia without sea-borne support'.*

Even before Buddha died in India (in about 483 BC) his religion had spread into China along the silk route, and overland into Burma. By 300 BC Buddhism was well established in south-east Asia. Most of the area, apart from North Vietnam, where the Chinese had settled, was occupied by two racial groups: the Mons in the north, who originated in Burma, and the Khmers from Cambodia.

Ports were established, the largest of which was Oc Eo, in what is now South Vietnam. Then it was part of the Khmer empire, as was Thailand. Archaeological excavations there have recovered a considerable quality of Chinese, Indian and Arab artefacts. Significantly, Roman coins and jewellery dating from the first century AD have also been found there. We know that the Romans had ventured as far as Cochin (south-west India) by this time, via the Persian Gulf. It is unlikely that Romans actually went in person to Oc Eo, but it is possible that, amongst the many things traded there on their behalf, were shrimp paste and fish sauce. Undeniably both were important Khmer ingredients, as they still are in all the countries of the region. These tastes were important in the Roman diet too (*see page 36*).

Meanwhile, in the Straits of Malacca, no major civilization had established itself, and neither Chinese nor Khmer influence had extended this far south. This allowed tribes people of Indian descent to settle in the Malaysian peninsula and on many of the Indonesian islands. They brought with them pepper, turmeric, ginger and a number of other Indian spices. Nutmeg and clove were already indigenous in the Malaccan islands, and coconut, an item they were already familiar with, grew everywhere. These ingredients became the major flavours of the area. They were equally popular in India's neighbour, Burma, and would have been well known to the country's major racial group of the time, the Mons.

At around this time, about 2000 years ago, we find the first evidence of a tribal race called T'ai or Thais, who were settled in the extreme south-west of China on the spice route to India. Under some pressure from a combination of other ethnic groups and the natural desire of the nomad to explore and to expand into new territories, Thais started to migrate southwards over the mountains. In about the ninth century, things became more urgent as warring Mongol hordes occupied Thai territory in southern China. What had for centuries been an insignificant trickle of Thai families or village groups, meandering southwards, became a torrent, and a whole race.

Most of the original Thais settled in the north of Thailand, in Lan Na and Chiang Rai, where they found little opposition from the small groups of resident hill tribes, whose descendants still live in this area. Rather more serious was organized opposition between those Mons and Khmers who occupied north and central Thailand respectively, but as is often the way with long established civilizations, both were in decline. By 1259 the northern Thais had driven the Mons back into Burma, and had set up Chiang Mai as their capital.

Another Thai group, further south, were able to drive the Khmer out of Thailand, and back into Cambodia. This group was known as the 'golden-skinned' or Shans, which in turn became Siamese. In 1238 they established their first great capital in the central plain on the banks of the mighty river Chao Praya. Called Sukhothai Siam (the dawn of happiness), they changed their language from a Chinese dialect to incorporate elements of Hindi, learned from the Mons, and developed the Thai alphabet, culture, food and Buddhist works of art. Under one great king, Siam grew until it occupied most of Indo-China and part of Burma, called the Shan state.

North of there, the Burmese Mons were at the peak of their civilization, when in 1280 the most famous of all medieval European voyagers, Marco Polo, made an overland voyage from Peking to their great capital city of Pagan, where Buddhist temples covered an area of 60 sq km. In his journals he likened their food to Indian.

Polo had for seventeen years been employed as an adviser to the then ruler of China, the Mongol emperor Kublai Khan. In 1292 he decided to sail home to Venice. Khan entrusted Polo to deliver one of his daughters as a wife for the Persian emperor. Their route took them around the coast of Indo-China, to Cambodia, in order to join an Indian vessel bound for Cochin. They were received by the Khmer king at Angkor Wat. It had become the capital of the Khmer empire as early as the sixth century, a role it was to maintain for 800 years. In its heyday it was an astonishing city, covering an area of 250 sq km, with a population of one million. It was a centre of trade, and rice in particular was mass-produced with the aid of an intricate irrigation network.

The well preserved remains of Angkor Wat survive to this day, beautiful, serene, ghost-like and uninhabited, of course, and virtually impossible to reach, thanks to the inhospitality of today's Khmer descendants. Surviving twelfth century bas reliefs show a more peaceful civilization, where pigs forage in paddy fields, bees make honey and the people are hard at work fishing, at their markets, gambling and cock fighting. Polo saw all this, and his journals frequently discuss Chinese food. He tells of enormous banquets for thousands of courtiers, where lacquered bowls overflowed with meats, rice, noodles and beans, soy and bamboo. Although Polo did not visit Siam, Chinese ingredients would certainly have been known to the Thais in Chiang Mai, where food is served on red lacquerware to this day.

Sukhothai was not to last. A rival king set up an alternative kingdom in 1358, with its capital Ayutthaya some 300km south of Sukhothai on the river Chao Praya. Within 200 years, Ayutthaya had become a trade centre to rival Baghdad and Peking, attracting foreign ambassadors and merchants from almost every country of the 'old world'. Its main exports included teak and rice. In return it received gold, weapons and textiles.

The Portuguese were the first Europeans to 'discover' Siam. Vasco da Gama, having pioneered the sea route to India round the Cape of Good Hope in 1498, had indeed found the source of pepper and many other spices, but not the fabled nutmeg and cloves. The search was still on. It was made more intense by the worry that arch rivals, Spain, would pip Portugal to the post by sailing round the world in the other direction. Afonso d'Albuquerque took up the baton, and in a series of exploratory moves, visited Bangladesh in 1510 and Siam in 1511, to find a mighty kingdom whose capital was Ayutthaya. He did this one year before finding the Malaccan islands, and their cloves and nutmeg. Portugal's most significant contributions to Siamese ingredients were the chilli, maize and egg-based confectionery.

Other Europeans were interested in the spice trade. By the mid-1600s the English, French and Dutch were all at the Ayutthaya court. Things came to a head in 1688 when the local Portuguese and Dutch allied themselves in an attempt to monopolize Siamese trade. Phaulkon, a Greek adviser to the then Siamese ruler, King Narai, called on the French to oust the Portuguese and Dutch. King Louis XIV of France took that to mean he could take over Siam, and he established French troops in garrisons up the river Chao Praya. As it happened, King Narai died, Phaulkon was executed and all Europeans were expelled from Siam. This over-reaction led to the beginning of Ayutthaya's decline and to a 'dark age' which lasted for 150 years. But it was almost certainly this which prevented Siam from becoming a colony.

Since the French were largely to blame for the expulsion, it is hardly surprising that they wrote somewhat sniffily about Thai food. Simon de la Loubere, a French Diplomat, wrote of a 'monotonous diet of copious rice mixed with dry fish, garlic and sweet herbs, to which a sauce of spices and water (*nam pla?*) is added'. Another banished Frenchman, missionary Nicholas Gervaise, describes shrimp paste as having a smell so pungent 'that it nauseates anyone not accustomed to it'.

Thai cooking clearly began to come together during the great court days of Ayutthaya, where the balance between the savoury of garlic and indigenous ginger (galangal) was matched with the salty taste of fish sauce and shrimp paste. The abundant piquancy of chilli was offset by the fragrance of native lemon grass and lime leaves. The herbs coriander and basil laced dishes together, their lightness of flavour matched by a lightness of cooking. Coconut made its appearance in certain dishes, but not in all. Dishes cooked with spicy pastes, influenced by Burma and Malaya, became curries quite unlike those of their Indian ancestry. Rice grains and rice noodles remained the staples.

By the time Europeans were allowed back into Siam (in 1828), they discovered that Ayutthaya was no more, and the court was well established in Bangkok under the Chakris dynasty. In their absence, they found that the Mons, who for two centuries had been warring with Siam, had , after a long siege, finally destroyed Ayutthaya, her king and most of her people in 1767. A young general, Taskin, had escaped with enough survivors, proclaimed himself king, and set up a new capital called Thon Buri, again on the river Chao Praya, well south of Ayutthaya. Thon Buri lasted just 15 years. Taskin went insane and was ousted in 1782 by a General Chakris who decided to build a new city on the east bank of the river opposite Thon Buri. He called it Bangkok – 'the city of the angles' – and named himself King Rama after the Hindu god. Bangkok signified the beginning of modern Siam. Rama became the first king of the Chakris Dynasty, whose descendant, King Rama IX, is the current monarch.

In Bangkok, Rama constructed a replica of Ayutthaya, complete with palaces, temples and canals. To replace the banished Europeans, he also encouraged a huge influx of Chinese traders, who soon established their enormous Bangkok China Town, and their monopolies on the trade of rice, salt and sugar. In 1826 the Siamese army had achieved a further victory over the warring Burmese. But this turned out to be different. Burma never invaded Siam again.

This was the new Siam the Europeans discovered. But how did Siam manage to become the only kingdom in the area to avoid being colonized? Thailand's monarchy was always powerful, its military disciplined and it may be this that saved it from British occupation.

While the Dutch, Portuguese and French were squabbling in Ayutthaya, the British East India Company had more pressing things on its mind than Siam. During the 140 year European exclusion between 1688 and 1828, Britain, through her East India Company, was building up her power in India. The French were contained to Pondicherry and the Portuguese to Goa, Diu and Daman. The Dutch were totally ousted. The Company wanted to expand trade into China, and needed to secure a southerly trade route from India. In 1786 Penang was acquired from the local sultan, enabling the British to springboard elsewhere. In 1795 she occupied Dutch Malacca, and Java in 1811, though these were returned when a treaty with the Dutch (signed in 1815) ended disputes over Indonesia. The establishment of Singapore in 1819 as a strategically placed major port, enabled the Company to control all Asian trade routes. Uses for Malaya which followed were the establishment of its tin and rubber industries.

Apart from brief periods of tenure in Siam, the Burmese Mons lost every war they started with the Siamese. This did not prevent them from invading Bengal, their neighbouring Indian state. The East India Company had no particular reason to want to occupy Burma, but it equally did not want Burma's intrusion so near to its most valuable port, Calcutta. So regular were Mons incursions between 1750 and 1820, that a considerable Indian army was kept on permanent readiness. It took three Anglo-Burmese wars, in 1824, 1852 and 1885, each won by Britain, before Burma was finally annexed to Britain.

Despite being pincered between two British territories, Siam had little to offer Britain either in assets or strategically. However, the French had made uncomfortably close acquisitions in Indo-China. Before long they were trying to influence King Rama IV (1851 to 1868), with, amongst other things, advice on the building of canals to expand Bangkok's waterway network. It was the time when the French were building the Suez Canal. They spotted a canal opportunity in Siam, at a point called the Kra Isthmus. Here, the coast to coast distance at the narrowest point is just 45km. This would cut 1600km off the India to China sea route, and it would bring prosperity to the canal's owner. It was a serious threat to Britain, however, as it would by-pass Singapore and lose them control of the Asian seas.

Fearing that the threat of forcible colonization was probably more likely from France than Britain, King Rama signed a treaty with both nations in 1855. France was given Cambodia, and Britain the Shan state of southern Burma in return for a promise to keep their hands off Siam. It did not, however, stop the French from continuing to promote their canal scheme. So strong was British opposition that they agreed to sign a further secret treaty with Siam in 1897, which gave Thailand a continued 'hands-off' promise from Britain, providing the canal was not built. Incidentally, speculation about this scheme continues to this day. It is frequently the subject of feasibility studies, but costs always prove to be prohibitive.

The Chakris dynasty was especially pro British. The kings all learned English, and Rama IV's other claim to fame was the employment of Anna Leonowens as governess to his children. Her autobiography was felt by Thais to depict the monarch in a derogatory manner. The book inspired a 1946 film, *Anna and the King of Siam*, which starred Irene Dunne and Rex Harrison. If that version was considered miscast and inaccurate, worse was to come from the offspring it spawned, a musical by Rodgers and Hammerstein which became the defamatory (in Thai eyes) 1956 movie, *The King and I* with Yul Brynner as an ignorant, naïve Rama IV. Anna (Deborah Kerr) was portrayed as being Rama's informed, nanny-knows-best educator in things British, not to mention having a fully fledged romance with the God King. Such a relationship would have been impossible. In Siam, no person was allowed to look at the monarch (grovelling face-down on the floor in his presence was not banned until years later), besides which, Rama IV had 35 wives and 83 children. Anna would have had her work cut out looking after her charges, and one of those was heir to the throne. Both films were banned from showing in Thailand. The Thai nation may not have seen them, but the rest of the world certainly did. Brynner was awarded an Oscar, and Thailand got an image which endured for decades. The other image which Thailand would prefer to forget was its association with the Japanese in World War II. This too was encapsulated in another Oscar winning movie, of which more later.

Back in 1782, soon after the court moved to Bangkok, Siamese food had been refined and improved in the royal kitchens. A range of dainty decorative finger foods had been invented using deep-frying as their cooking medium. Pretty titles such as Emerald Parcels, Golden Bags and Fire Crackers (krathuk) (see Chapter 2), were some of the results. Refined salads also entered the repertoire (see Chapter 4) and a great deal of attention was focused on producing colourful desserts, such as Ruby Eyes. Mainstream dishes such as soups, entrées, curries, rice and noodles had remained virtually unchanged for centuries, unaffected by outside influences, but recipes were undoubtedly worked upon until the balance of flavours was perfected. Presentation was given a complete new look, unique to Thai food to this day. At the dextrous hands of the royal cooks, a whole new art-form evolved, involving garnishing. It centred on fruit and vegetable carving and was considered so prestigious that all daughters-at-court, from the highest princess downwards, spent their early years learning it, along with flower arranging and doll-making. There has been little or no change to Thai food since those days.

Gastronomy, and cooking itself, was considered important enough for more than one monarch to profess to be an expert. King Rama V was said to be a dab hand in the kitchen. Even though he had been Anna's principal charge, it is hard to imagine the God King in his pinny at the stove!

What is on record is that the British ambassador of the time, Sir John Bowring, was a Siamese food aficionado. His diaries from 1855 contain recipes for shrimp paste and Siamese curries.

The Chakris dynasty continued to bring western ideas into Siam, ruling with continuity and dignity. Medicine, the printing press, roads, railways, and humane laws were established. Slavery was eventually abolished and women were no longer required to shave their heads. Schools and universities were founded, as were libraries and the post office. American missionaries arrived, and with them the potato and the tomato made their first appearances in Siam. Surnames were introduced for the first time, so too was football. Driving on the left, as in Britain was made official. And that Rama VI was pro-British was amply demonstrated in World War I, when he sent Siamese troops to fight alongside the Allies in the trenches in 1917.

Despite all these reforms, the monarchy was still all-powerful, and moves to establish a democratic parliament eventually came to fruition in 1932, with an army-led bloodless coup. Siam was renamed Thailand. King Rama VII was retained as monarch, but with considerably reduced powers.

The world was in too much turmoil itself to care about Thailand. America and Europe were reeling from the effects of the Depression. German belligerence was re-emerging. So it was in Japan, whose people, hit especially hard by the Depression, began to believe that they were the natural leaders in Asia. They attacked China in 1937, and the outbreak of World War II gave them the excuse they needed to occupy Indo-China, in the belief that acquisition of the rubber and petroleum industries would guarantee Japanese domination. The Thai government chose to side with Japan in 1940, and did not oppose Japanese occupation of the country in 1941. Indeed, they went further and 'officially' declared war on the Allies, although this was never officially recognized because the Thai ambassador in Washington refused to deliver the document to the White House. This lucky event gave Thailand allied status after the war.

The Japanese, however, raced on to occupy the entire Pacific Rim, the windfall prize being the unexpectedly easy surrender of the massive British garrison on Singapore, as well as those in Burma and Malaya. Many of these unfortunate souls became POWs and were set to hard labour as slaves, their most notorious project being the building of a railway to link Singapore to India. Most of the track already existed, but a 400km stretch was missing mostly in Thailand, and in Burma. The Japanese saw the achievement of this as vital to their planned occupation of India. They put 100,000 prisoners-of-war to work, literally to carve the route through the mountains and valleys. The job took just 16 months and cost 16,000 prisoners their lives, earning the job its hideously apt name, the 'Death Railway'. Many bridges were required, but one in particular at Kanchanaburi, some 130km north-west of Bangkok, passed into infamy where it crosses the local river, the Mae Nam Khwae Yai. It was David Lean's Oscar winning 1957 film, *The Bridge on the River Kwai*, which through Alec Guiness' heroic role, focused the world's attention on this attrocity, although few people were aware, then or now, that Thailand was the location.

Post-war Thailand went quietly about its business, with its current monarch, King Rama IX, succeeding to the throne in 1946. But necessary though it may have been to reduce the power of the monarchy, it has

farmers, on their never-ending paddy fields and fruit orchards. Into the Chao Praya flow many small tributaries, which make the plains the food bowl of Thailand.

SOUTHERN THAILAND

This area is on the long, narrow isthmus which shares its northern border with Burma, and its southern border with Malaya. Its dense rainforest jungles earn it the name Pak Thai, and give it a humid, hot climate. Rubber, coconut, pineapples and cashews are the main crops.

The further south you go, the more Moslems and mosques you encounter. Hence, you will find lamb and mutton in place of pork. Sheep meat is disliked elsewhere in Thailand.

Seafood is abundant, with rock lobster from Phuket (a main tourist beach area) particularly prized. Two particular curries originate from this area, both derived from Malay Indian ancestry: *Panaeng* with its peanut base, and *Mussaman* (Moslem) curry which contains the widest repertoire of Indian spices. They like it hot down south, the area coming second only to the north-east.

One flavour not enjoyed elsewhere is a particularly bitter taste given by a local bean variety (*sa-taw*).

HAWKER FOOD

NO BOOK on Thai food would be complete without mention of one of Thailand's most buoyant industries – her food hawkers.

In Victorian times every British city had them – sole traders wandering on foot from door to door and person to person calling their wares, be it fruit, meat, milk or snacks. Such services may be memories in the West – but they are very much alive and thriving in Thailand.

No other country on Earth has such a diverse and prolific street food industry as Thailand. Hawkers appear in great numbers all over the country. They sell all manner of Thai food cooked and cold. Each hawker specializes in a particular item or dish. Some have stalls at markets, while the majority are mobile. Their shop is portable. All their ingredients and tools, and even the heating system, alight while on the move, may be contained in a simple basket, or suspended between two trays hanging from a yoke. Or they may be built into a wheeled handcart or trolley.

At one time, some hawkers sold their wares (traditionally noodles) from teak boats on Bangkok's *klongs* (canals). With the infilling of many canals in recent years these boats are all but extinct. But their hawkers aren't, and though now land-based, their trolley, either static or mobile, has retained the canal tradition. It is boat shaped.

The size of the hawker's unit and the amount of clutter (utensils and ingredients) needed will vary, and gives the clue to what speciality is being prepared and cooked. A butane cylinder may support a frying pan or a wok for stir-fries or deep-fries. I've seen enormous two handled brass woks full of bubbling oil in the thronging pavements being narrowly avoided by speeding passers-by. Clay pots containing coals heat curries and stews. A 'steamboat' (*see page 71*) may signify a soup. Other hawkers have glass cases built on to their trolleys, in which they display their food. These may be heated or chilled. The fact is that you'll find literally any of the recipes from this book being prepared and cooked on the street at a fraction of the cost you'd pay for it at a nearby restaurant.

This is not the only reason why they are so popular. It is part of the Thai city dweller's *joie de vivre*, or *sanuk*, to nose about (*pai thiaw*) to see what's happening. Whether they are at leisure, or busy office workers on a meal-break, they love their hawkers. Queues throng around them all day long, and much of the night, and they proliferate in any public places – at markets, on busy pavements, outside shops, office blocks, cinemas, at railway stations and bus terminals.

Households are not deprived of their hawkers either. In an age-old tradition, bevies of vendors ply the residential streets all day long, in a door-to-door trek announced by as wide a variety of songs, calls, shouts, croaks, honks, hoots, rings and clacks as the ready meals and snacks they sell.

RESTAURANTS

O NE LEGACY Bangkok and other Thai cities do have is a restaurant tradition that goes back a long time. Restaurants were, in all probability, 'invented' in China. Marco Polo visited China twice, briefly in 1265 and in 1275, staying there the second time for seventeen years. In his journals he described thronged streets, market stalls, tradesmen, food hawkers, restaurants and tea-houses. At around this time, as we have seen, the original Thais were migrating en masse from their homelands in south China and settling in northern Thailand.

Much of their early culture and language was Chinese, and the notion of communal eating whether 'on-the-hoof', from market traders or seated at the tea-house is a tradition carried on to modern times. Certainly, eating is a popular activity and a thriving trade in Thailand. It takes place at any price level, from expensive restaurants to cheap cafés and to prove it, in Bangkok for example, there are over 11,000 restaurants. Bangkok is a twenty-four-hour city, and though many of the big restaurants shut before midnight, you can certainly buy food elsewhere all night. Being perpetual grazers, this especially suits those Thais who like to eat little and often. Markets operate day and night, and the streets are alive with food hawkers, each of whom specializes in just one dish or item, be it fried, steamed, barbecued, rice or noodles.

Bangkok's Thai restaurants have flair. They have the biggest restaurant in the world (Tumnak Thai) with an astonishing 3,500 seats, and you still have to book to guarantee a seat. Waitering is done very efficiently on roller skates. Thailand also has establishments called seafood restaurants where the diners select their own food from a supermarket section, then have it cooked and delivered to their table. They also have some wonderfully serene restaurants in traditional teak houses, where the diner sits lotus-style to be served by staff in traditional costumes, often to the accompaniment of the soft dulcet tones of Thai music from wooden xylophones.

Many Thais are emigrating to the United States, to Europe and to Australia, resulting in a Thai restaurant boom in all these countries. Nowhere is this boom spreading more quickly than in Britain. In a country whose ethnic restaurant scene has been dominated for several decades by Indo-Bangladeshi curry houses and Chinese restaurants, it is not surprising that Thai restaurants did not exist here before 1980. Today every major town has at least one Thai restaurant, and a remarkable growth is taking place.

At the beginning of 1994, Britain had 300 Thai restaurants. By the end of 1995 there were 500. At the supermarket, Thai ingredients and ready meals are increasing in market share. The British, it seems, have taken to Thai food.

This is a book I have been wanting to write for some years. I hope it will give you a greater insight into one of the world's most interesting and delicious cuisines.

It's time to step into the kitchen...

CHAPTER 1

THAI CULINARY WORKSHOP

A s REGULAR readers of my books will know, it is a tradition of mine to call the first chapter 'The Workshop', in this case the 'Thai Culinary Workshop'. The reason for this is that, like any workshop, it's the depository of a number of unrelated items which are vital to Thai cooking and which appear throughout the other chapters. It includes brief notes about main ingredients including oils, herbs, spices, coconut, fish sauce, noodles, rice and wonton wrappers, amongst others. There are also nine very important recipes for pastes, stocks, crispy garlic and onion, tamarind purée, and for want of a better place to put it, the decorative egg net.

I suggest you spend a few hours in your workshop (your kitchen) and make up batches for subsequent use. This will make it quicker and easier to use some of the main recipes in the book. Cooking larger batches and freezing surplus helps to contain smells, particularly from garlic, and labour and washing up to one occasion now and again, which you will find enjoyable rather than a chore.

Before we get down to cooking, I have given information about the equipment you will need to cook Thai food, how to freeze and keep it, how to prepare ingredients, weights and measures, portions, presentation and serving, and the all important advice on what to drink with your meal. I recommend you read the following section first. Pour yourself a glass of something, settle down and read this chapter in comfort!

KITCHEN IMPLEMENTS

A S WE HAVE seen in the introduction, Thai food has evolved over centuries. Like Chinese and Indian cooking, its techniques are basically simple ones. To this day the majority of Thais are villagers, and cooking techniques have not changed to take modern appliances into account. It is only in the larger cities, where constant electricity and running water are now taken for granted, that the trappings of 'modern life' are appearing. The instant hob, the oven, the microwave, the fridge and the freezer are all new to Thai cuisine. Even more so are gadgets such as rice cookers and electric spice mills. But for 85 per cent of Thailand's population, stone grinders and wood (or meths) burning stoves are the norm.

Cooking utensils are confined to two-handled woks (traditionally made from brass) for deep-frying and stir-frying, and metal or earthenware pots for slow cooking. There are many bamboo items – steamers, spoons, strainers, containers and so on, as well as a large chopping board (often circular and deep, made from the trunk of a tree) and, of course, sharp knives. Some households have a brass steamer used for Tom Yam soup (*see page 73*).

All of this traditional Thai cooking equipment can now be purchased in Britain and very attractive it is, too. I have used many of these traditional items in the pictures throughout this book. However, for day-to-day cooking, few of us want anything other than convenience, speed, efficiency and the most hygenic method. We really don't want to bother with wood stoves (apart from charcoal on the barbecue, perhaps) nor with time-consuming hand grinding. If the oven, the grill or non-stick pans can do the job as well as traditional items, let's use them. Most of us will already have the necessary implements and utensils. If you don't already own them I do recommend that you purchase at least a couple of good quality steel woks.

I prefer the one-handled wok to the two-handled. It is less easy to burn your fingers. You need a couple about 30cm in diameter. Woks need 'seasoning' when new. Firstly, you must scrub off the machine oil which protects them. Next, you must 'burn them' in, by drying them on the stove. Then oil them and burn the oil in (a smoky business which is better done outside, perhaps when the barbecue is going). Repeat with a second oiling. To clean, they say you should never scour the patina off a wok. Often this is acceptable, but if you have burnt in some food, it is hygenic to scour it off. You may need to season the wok again. Woks work well on gas, electric and Aga type hobs, especially if you obtain a wok ring. Woks do not work well on ceramic and halogen stoves. They tend to cut off automatically because the wok base is smaller than the ring diameter.

Here is a list of the utensils you will need to cook the recipes in this book.

KNIVES

CHOPPING BOARD

MIXING BOWLS – large, medium and small

SIEVES

LARGE, SLOTTED SPOON for use in a deep-fryer

DEEP-FRYER

CASSEROLE DISH(ES) – 2.25 to 2.75 litres

SAUCEPANS WITH LIDS – 3.5 litres, 2.25 litres, 1.4 litres

OVEN TRAYS

GRILL TRAY with wire rack

BAMBOO OR METAL STEAMER – a 20cm or larger pan with a perforated inner pan and tight-fitting lid (or a well fitting sieve over a pan with a lid can be substituted).

STEEL WOK(S) – 30cm diameter

WOK RING(S)

ELECTRIC TOOLS

FOOD PROCESSOR OR BLENDER

COFFEE GRINDER – unlike Indian, few Thai recipes require spices to be ground. But for those that do, a small electric coffee grinder is most effective. Do not overload it beyond the halfway mark. A wipe with a damp cloth leaves the grinder ready to grind coffee beans without tainting them.

KEEPING THAI FOOD

LIKE ITS Chinese counterparts, Thai food is intended to be cooked then eaten more or less immediately. This is because in Thailand the heat and humidity would quickly make the food go off, and there were no fridges or freezers until quite recently. Even now only middle and upper classes own them. And even now most prefer not to keep food for reheating. However, with refrigeration, many of the recipes in this book will not be any the worse for keeping overnight, or even longer. Provided that the raw ingredients are absolutely fresh, not frozen, and are cooked immediately, and provided that the dish is cooled rapidly after cooking, then covered and placed in the fridge at once, the food should be safe for up to 48 hours.

As a general rule, any meat or poultry dish can be served immediately after cooking, or a few hours later, or even a day or two later. The taste and texture of the dish will change as marination takes place. This usually means the flavours will become blander and the principal ingredient softer. It's up to you which you prefer. Vegetables, in my opinion, taste better served straight after cooking, but some of these will keep too. Rice does not generally keep, although you may get away with keeping it for a day, or maybe more. Fresh chutneys should always be served fresh.

Common sense must prevail when keeping any food. If you prefer to keep food, I would suggest you observe the following points:

1   Do not keep fish or shellfish dishes.
2   If you intend to keep a meat dish for a day or two, undercook it slightly by cutting back the timings by a few minutes. You will obtain a better texture when reheating – simply simmer until ready.
3   Use common sense about which vegetables will keep.
4   Keep away from warmth, and preferably in a fridge.
5   Use a cover or film.
6   Inspect meat or chicken after 24 hours. Smell and taste it. It should look firm and good.
7   Heat must be applied relatively quickly when reheating (as opposed to slowly). Simmer and stir for at least 10 minutes (especially for meat or poultry) and before serving check that the food is hot right through.
8   During reheating, taste, and if it needs a boost of a little more flavouring, add it early so that it cooks in well.
9   Do not use if you even suspect it may be going off. Forty-eight hours is a long time for any dish to sit around, and freezing is a much safer method of storing.

FREEZING

To the Western householder, the freezer is a mandatory item in the workshop/kitchen. Like the fridge, it too has its uses and drawbacks.

The main point about home freezing is to preserve seasonal items for use out of season. I like to do this with some things and not with others. I prefer to freeze my own sweetcorn – it tastes so much better than the commercial versions. On the other hand, I think bought frozen peas are in many cases better than home-frozen ones. You can freeze fruit and vegetables raw, exactly as they are when picked or purchased (cleaning and discarding unwanted matter first). I often do this, but the textbooks advise that you should cook the subject matter first, at least blanch it, to remove bacteria and gases. It's up to you.

Freezing comes in to its own with the preservation of cooked foods, and it is ideal for some complete Thai dishes. Freezing can change the taste of a dish – it's like a long marination. It will soften meats and vegetables and tends to intensify certain aromatic spices, though the overall taste will become blander.

Here are a few common sense freezer observations:

1   Use only fresh ingredients, not items that have come from the supermarket freezer, if these have been thawed.
2   Choose your subject carefully. Some ingredients are not suitable for freezing. Items with a high water content change markedly in structure when they thaw, their texture becoming unpleasant. Meat and poultry are excellent, as are all lentil dishes. Some vegetables work well – aubergines, peas, beans, carrots and mashed potatoes, for example. Most soft fruit and vegetables and whole potatoes are not as successful. Fish and seafood work well, too. Rice is satisfactory, but I can never see the point – it takes so little time to make fresh rice and it has a better taste and texture.
3   Always undercook a dish destined for the freezer by a few minutes to allow for 'tenderizing' in the freezing process and reheating.
4   Take out any large whole spices before freezing, especially cassia, cardamoms and cloves as they tend to become a bit astringent.
5   Get the dish into the freezer as soon as it is cold. Do not freeze if the food has been kept warm for a long time or reheated, especially chicken. There is a risk of bacterial contamination.
6   Be aware that spicy food can taint other foods, so pack in a plastic container with an airtight lid.
7   Label contents with their description and freezing date.
8   Use within 3 months.
9   When reheating ensure that the dish is thoroughly hot and cooked through.
10 You may find the flavouring has gone a little bland, so taste and cook in more flavourers as needed.
11 Finally, never ever freeze, then thaw and then refreeze an item.

ICE CUBE MOULD

C ERTAIN HIGHLY flavoured items can be made in bulk and frozen in small portions. 'Magic paste' (*see page 42*) containing garlic, and shrimp paste (*see page 36*) are two examples. My solution is to keep an ice cube mould specifically for the purpose. Freeze for 24 hours then transfer to a suitable tub or double bag to contain the aromas.

PREPARING THAI INGREDIENTS

T HIS IS STATING the obvious, but please do prepare all your ingredients before you start cooking. And by that I mean assemble any bottled or tinned items (open the tin). Wash, trim and chop fresh items as the recipe states. Weigh and measure as required, and have everything to hand. Once the cooking begins, one's concentration should be with timings and stirrings, not with locating lost items.

PORTIONS

E XCEPT WHERE stated, most of the recipes in this book serve four people with average appetites. I normally allow about 700g (25oz) of the principal ingredients of a main course, (after it is shorn of anything inedible) for four servings. Usually there is about 225g (8oz) of extra items in a dish, to give about 225g per person in total.

For an accompanying main-course dish allow 75g (3oz) per person, and for rice allow 50 to 75g (2 to 3oz) uncooked weight.

These quantities are given for guidance only. Appetites vary enormously. One person may eat two or even three times as much as another. So, as with all aspects of cooking, common sense should prevail.

Having said all that, rather than weigh things, it is often easier to visualize exactly what each diner will eat. Think of potatoes, for example. You'll eat two, she'll eat three, Uncle Fred six, Aunty Mary one, and so on.

If you wish to cook for one person, either scale down the quantities or use the freezer. If you wish to cook for more than four, scale up. Taste and adjust as you go. If you feel a particular dish needs more flavouring, add some. Flexibility is, as always, the key.

PRESENTATION AND SERVING

FOOD IS ALL important to the Thai people. Their equivalent of 'how are you?' literally means 'have you eaten rice?' and their summons to the table, *kin khao*, literally translates as 'eat rice'.

Rice appears at nearly every Thai meal. At breakfast time it is Khao Tom (*page 75*). This is rice soup with shredded meat or chicken, prawn, garlic, egg and pickles. The day can also end with this dish.

Lunch is generally an 'on-the-hop' one dish meal. If it isn't a rice dish, it would be noodles such as Pad Thai (*page 158*), meaning literally 'Thai stir-fry'. Its beauty is that it can contain anything and everything to accompany the noodles. It is also very quick to make and very filling.

Dinner is, as in most countries, a more considered meal. A traditional dinner, attended by a number of diners, should consist of a rice dish, a soup or two, a herby or spicy salad, a curry or stew, a grilled or stir-fried item(s) and a vegetable dish, followed by dessert and/or fruit. There would, of course, be plenty of chutneys and dips. All dishes would be served at once, allowing the diner freedom of choice in the order of eating. Most of the dishes are served in bowls. The rice would occupy the largest one.

The selection of dishes should give pleasing colour and texture combinations, as well as balance between each dish in piquancy, wet and dry, sweet and sour and creaminess. There is also a philosophical concept found all over the south-east Asia which involves 'hot' and 'cool' food. This is not to do with temperature or piquancy, but is to do with the internal persona of the individual. This philosophy is found in India and China as well as Thailand. But it is complex. What is 'hot' in one country may be 'cool' in the next. For example, eggs are 'hot' food in Bangladesh but 'cool' in Thailand.

For the meals you will make from this book, you can serve them in one course if you wish, but it is more conventional in the West to serve courses, which suits Thai food well. My menu suggestions on pages XII to XVI give a number of examples.

As to actual serving, use decorative plates or bowls to serve each dish in. The diner will require a plate and a soup bowl. Cutlery should consist of a spoon and fork. Traditionally, Thais use the fork to load the spoon, off which they eat. They regard eating from the fork as bad mannered (in the way that we regard eating from the knife). Knives, by the way, are not supplied since all Thai food is cut into bite-size pieces before cooking. You might prefer to use a knife and fork.

Prior to the twentieth century, incidentally, cutlery was not used at all in Thailand, the food being eaten with the right hand, as in India. It is quite acceptable to eat starters and very crispy items with the fingers. Chopsticks and Chinese soup spoons are only used with noodle dishes.

Food decoration, in the form of garnishes and 'set pieces', has become an art form unmatched in any other international cuisine. At the restaurant, or for an important home meal, it would be inconceivable to put a dish on the table ungarnished. (*page 175*).

WHAT TO DRINK

APART FROM the Thai Moslem population in the south, most Thais have no rules about alcohol. There is a thriving beer industry, the most popular bottled brands (and strongest at 6 per cent alcohol content) being Singha lager with Kloster and Amarit (both 4.7 per cent) also available. Called *bia* in Thai, they are all subject to high tax (about two-thirds of its cost) making a 660ml (20fl oz) bottle cost half a day's pay for a manual labourer.

Thai-produced spirits are equally heavily taxed. Whisky is the most prevalent. Made from rice, it is quite unlike Scotch, having a bitter-sweet taste. Thai rum is more syrupy. There are no home produced wines.

At meal times, cold water or tea is popular, as is whisky with water. Fruit juices of all kinds are readily available and very popular all over Thailand. As to what you and I might like to drink with our Thai meal, the choice is wide open from any of the above. My preference is for wine, and since there are considerable similarities between Thai food and Indian, in that both contain spices, chillies and strong flavourings, I can do no better than to quote celebrated wine journalist and critic David Wolfe, who says in the Curry Club Good Curry Restaurant Guide (*see page ii*):

'*Diluted spirits are not to everyone's taste nor are fruit drinks. Water is boring, and reacts with some spices to give a metallic twang at the back of the throat. Nor is copious water with rice a good idea. Beer tastes better, but the large volumes can be bloating; and for my palate, beer however good, lacks the depth of flavour to match Indian spices – although it cleans the palate effectively.*

'So for me, and many others, wine is ideal – providing it has masses of flavour. A delicate Muscadet or Beaujolais is delicious; even sweeter wines like German Riesling can be refreshing at the right time and place. But wine, even white wine, is not a thirst-quencher. On the contrary, its high alcohol content makes it dehydrating.

'Since white wines generally have less flavour, it must be red to stand up to the spices and herbs. Most wine books say fine wine is spoiled by chillies. But in my own experience, this is not so. The wine and spices do not argue face to face, but slide past each other. As the wine flavour momentarily takes over the palate 'forgets' the chillies, then the chillies return and the wine is forgotten.'

David has put forward an original and interesting concept. Personally, I enjoy red wine with just about everything, curry included. I particularly enjoy the blackberry tastes of St -Emilion and Pauillac or the resonance of a good Australian Shiraz, or the body of Châteauneuf-du-Pape. Spanish and Chilean reds often support curry well and are reasonably priced.

In practice these days, car drivers find themselves unable to drink more than a token. I have found the perfect solution in the 'spritzer' – a combination of one part dry white wine to three parts sparkling mineral water. Mind you, this in no way substitutes for my favourite tipple – champagne, pink or white – preferably vintage! Cheers!

OILS

LIKE CHINESE, Thai cooking always uses light, unsaturated oils such as sunflower, soya, vegetable or corn oil. Never use olive oil or nut oils, ghee or lard in Thai cooking. The former are too strong in flavour and the latter simply do not exist in Thailand. Just occasionally you can use sesame oil (though it is not traditional) and I've used butter in a few recipes in this book. Again, butter is not a traditional Thai food item. Neither, for that matter are milk, yoghurt, cream or cheese. As in Chinese food, dairy products simply do not appear in most Thai recipes.

HERBS AND LEAVES

ONE OF THE greatest aspects of Thai cooking is its use of herbs. Basil and coriander are the most popular and they are used quite prolifically in recipes. Mint (spearmint) is also used.

BASIL

Basil had the distinction of being nominated the 'king' of herbs in ancient times. Indigenous to east Asia, it had reached Europe by the time of the Greek empire. It was so revered that it got its name from Greek royalty (*basilikos* meaning royal). Indeed, sources state that only the sovereign (*basileus*) was permitted to eat it. And to discourage the public from experimenting, rumours abounded that any association with basil could turn the user into a scorpion!

Today, there are 40 varieties of basil available world wide. Most common in Britain is sweet basil (*Ocimum basilicum*). Two varieties of purple basil (purple ruffle and dark opal) are available. A pretty beetroot in colour, the leaves of the former are quite deeply serrated, and the latter less so, but its fragrance is more spicy, veering towards gingery.

Three main varieties of Thai basil are used in their cooking. Thai sweet basil (*Ocimum basilicum horapha*) or *bai horapa* in Thai, is the most widely used. It is slightly spicier than the Western variety with a strong hint of fennel seed or aniseed. Its appearance is different from Western sweet basil. Its leaves are a little smaller with a pointed tip, and can have a slight purply tinge. It is often available with small, edible purple flowers, as can be seen on the rice dish in the photograph adjacent to page 00/p5.

Holy basil (*Ocimum sanctum*) is also commonly used in Thai cooking. It is called *bai grapao* in Thailand, and *tulsi* in India, where it is used in Hindu religious ceremonies (hence the name). Its leaves are larger than *horapa* – and about the same size as our sweet basil – although the edges are serrated (whereas ours are smooth) and they are less shiny, perhaps paler than Western basil, giving it the further occasional names 'light green' or 'pale' basil. *Grapao* has a hot or peppery taste. For this reason it is sometimes called 'hot' basil and it is popular in Thai curries, and, strangely enough, it is always specified for frogs' legs (*page 98*).

The third variety is *bai manglak*, bush basil (*Ocimum canum*) or Greek basil. It is also sometimes called 'hairy' basil because its leaves have tiny hairs. The leaves are the smallest of the three Thai basil varieties (averaging 4cm in length) and are quite pointed. *Manglak* has a distinctively lemony flavour which makes it a gorgeous garnish with salads. Thais also use it with glass noodle, soup and fish curry. Its lemony flavour leads to many a misnomer. Manglak is not lemon basil (*Ocimum citriodorum*) nor is it Italian basil, though both can be substituted.

I have found in my detailed research that basil suffers the same problem as chilli. It frequently gets misnamed in cookery books. Several

Thai cookbooks have muddled the descriptions of *horapa* and *grapao*, for example. And seed growers can get muddled, too. And neither lemon balm nor balsam is basil (one isn't even a herb!).

The safest bet is to order seeds by the Latin (botanical) name, and the Thai name at the Thai shop for their three basil varieties.

CORIANDER

Coriander (*Coriandrum sativum*) is now widely available in the West. Its musky candle wax flavour is decidedly an acquired taste, but once acquired one cannot live without it.

Incidentally, like basil the word coriander also derives from a Greek word. Coriander has humbler connotations. The word is *koris*, a bug (actually said to be a bed bug, with a particularly foetid smell). Not being an expert in such matters, as I'm sure you aren't either, I can't confirm its validity.

The whole of the coriander plant is used in Thai cooking. Leaves, stems and roots are all used, as can be seen in the 'magic' paste recipe on page 42.

If you want the appearance of coriander, but not its musk, use flat-leaf parsley (*Petroselinum sativum*). Since the two leaves are similar, the trick to identification at the greengrocer is to crush a leaf in your fingers. Only coriander has the musky smell.

LEMON GRASS
Takrai

Most of us are familiar with the smell of lemon grass (*Cymbopogon citratus*). It is sweetish and, in my view, only vaguely lemony, but very distinctively fragrant. It is widely used in soaps and on face towels.

The plant itself is indispensable to Thai cooking. It is a grass, but only the thin stalky bulbous end is used. Now readily available in the West, we get to purchase the bulbous end and a little of the green stalk in pieces about 25cm long (the thickest part of the end being about $1\frac{1}{2}$cm in diameter).

To use, pull off any tough outer stem, cut off the bottom $\frac{1}{2}$cm to 1cm, and cut off the upper stalk where it changes from white to green; this should leave you with a piece 10cm to 15cm in length.

There are two cutting methods referred to throughout this book:

THE TASSEL

Place the lemon grass, prepared as above, flat on the chopping board, holding the thinner upper end. Cut longways for about three-quarters of their length, several times. This will create a one piece tassel. This is used to infuse the lemon grass into the cooking, the tassel giving maximum surface area. It can be used as a garnish but not eaten in this form.

CROSSCUT

Having prepared the lemon grass as mentioned above, make only one cut longways, as described in the tassel. Then crosscut the diameter of the bulbous end toward the green end. As as option, this can be slightly diagonal. This creates thin semicircles. Now break these apart to create half moons. They resemble 'finger nails'.

Add them to the recipe as directed. In this form they are edible, the thinner the better. Fresh lemon grass can be frozen. It is also available crosscut dried and in powder form. Both forms need an hour or two reconstituting in water and are nothing like as good, of course, as fresh.

BOTTLED LEMON GRASS

The best part of the stalks are available bottled about 7cm to 8cm long preserved in sterilised lemon grass water. These are the best substitute for fresh and can be used in tassels or crosscut (see above). The liquid can be used too.

LIMES AND LIME LEAVES

There are two different types of lime found in Thailand. The 'regular' or common lime is green or yellow ovate ball with a smooth skin and sharp juice (*citrus aurantifolia*) or *manao* in Thai.

The more commonly used Thai lime is harder to find in the West, but is worth seeking out at the Thai shop. Called the wild lime (*citrus hytrix*), *kaffir* or *makroot* in Thai, it is about the same size and shape as the common lime, but it has a knobbly skin. Its juice is much sweeter, as is its pith and skin. Both are used in Thai cooking, whereas the common lime is rarely called for. This commonly leads to mistakes in certain Thai cookery books, which call for liberal amounts of lime juice and/or peel. This creates a sharp taste which you'd never find in Thailand. It is the kaffir lime you need. It is a relative of the bergamot family.

LIME LEAF

Lime leaves are from the kaffir tree. They are another secret weapon in the Thai culinary repertoire. Called *bai-makroot*, and used like bay leaves, they are wonderful if you can get them, but have no substitute if you can't. They are shiny, dark green, the leaves are more or less circular, about 4cm in diameter, or smaller. Their peculiarity is that they grow in pairs, one above the other. Their branches have sharp thorns like rose tree branches. They are available dried (acceptable if you can't get fresh ones), or powdered (useless as far as I'm concerned). Fresh is best, of course, from the Thai shop. They can be used whole or cut into the thinnest strips (chifonade strips) after removing the stem. Whole leaves are inedible, the shreds delicious to eat. Lime leaves can be frozen.

MINT
Bai saranae

Mint is far too aromatic and exciting to be passed up by Thai cooks, although it has to be said that its appearance is as a support act rather than the star (this role is taken by basil). Spearmint appears in some recipes in this book.

NON-EDIBLE LEAVES

In any ancient cuisine you will always find a 'waste-not-want-not' culture coupled with huge ingenuity. In Thailand, a small example of this is the continued use of two non-edible leaves in cooking.

BANANA LEAF
Bai kruay

The banana leaf has a number of roles. The banana tree is a kind of palm tree, whose leaf is long and wide, pliable (almost rubbery), yet durable and easily disposable. It can be used as a table mat, as in India, or as a cooking container (*see pages 52 and 118*).

PANDANUS LEAF
Bai toey

Although virtually unknown in the West, the pandanus leaf (*Pandanus odorus*) or screwpine, is widely used in Malaysian, Indonesian and Thai cooking. The leaf is about 50cm long and 5cm wide and is available from Thai shops.

Its oil forms the basis of Indian *kewra*, a highly scented cooking water. Though inedible itself, it can be used like bay leaf in Thai soups and in rice (and I have given it as an option in certain recipes in those chapters). It has a further resourceful use for the Thais as the knotted container for deep-fried chicken in the splendidly named Emerald Chicken Parcel (*page 56*).

SPICES

UNLIKE INDIAN cuisine, the spice list for Thai cooking is minimal. Very few Thai recipes call for spices. Even most Thai curries only call for coriander, cummin, paprika, chilli and turmeric, and not of all those in each recipe. That is apart from the wonderful Mussaman Curry (*page 144*), which is the only recipe in this book to require whole coriander, cumin seeds, cloves, star aniseed, cardamoms, cassia bark and bay leaf. Sesame is another rarity (*page 85*). But turmeric, ground and root (*page 41*) makes more frequent appearances. White pepper is very prevalent, and fresh green pepper is popular too.

CHILLI
Nam prig

LAST BUT by no means least in the spice department – chilli is certainly not 'least' to any normal Thai. Many Thai dishes are laced with chilli to incendiary level. Indeed the Thais have bred a tiny chilli which is one of the hottest in the world. We'll meet it later.

It seems inconceivable that there was once Thai cuisine without chillies. But that certainly was the case. Chillies, having been 'discovered' in the Americas post-Columbus, were brought to Thailand by the Portuguese in the sixteenth century.

The rest, as in India, is history. Chilli is the seed-carrying pod or fruit of a perennial shrub, whose botanical name is *Capsicum*. The principal attribute of chilli is its piquancy or 'hot' taste. The level of 'heat' varies from zero in the familiar Capsicum sweet pepper (also called bell pepper, as I have done in this book) to ten out of ten in a few species. In Thailand, the hottest variety clocks in at a huge nine out of ten. There are a number of other chilli varieties in Thailand. Here are the principal ones in descending order of 'heat' level (hottest to mildest):

Habanero or Scotch bonnet (not Thai)	10
Thai miniature, *prig kee noo* (literally 'rat droppings')	8 to 9
1 to 2cm cayenne – red or green	7 to 8
Spur pepper 4 to 6cm, *prig chee fa* (literally points to sky – grows upwards), red, green, yellow or orange	5
African snub or Jalapeño *prig kaset* (literally 'weak pepper'), green	3 to 4
Bell pepper, *prig toom*, red, yellow, green, orange	0

COCONUT

The coconut is the largest nut in the the world, which grows prolifically in the eastern tropics. It is widely used in Thai cooking, though not in every region. For example, it is not used in the Issan north-eastern inland district. This vast seed, growing atop a palm tree, is enclosed with a thick fibrous circular casing, green in colour. It is de-husked with a cleaver – to reveal the more familiar brown hairy ovate coconut, with three small depressions or 'eyes'. Inside is coconut water – a pleasant-tasting transparent liquid. When buying a fresh coconut, shake it to ensure it is full of liquid. The more liquid it has, the fresher it is. A coconut without liquid, or with mouldy or wet 'eyes', should not be used. The liquid can be drunk or used in stock. The all important part of the coconut in culinary terms is its 'flesh'. This is a 1cm bright white layer, coating the inside husk of the sphere. To reach it, we must 'open' the coconut.

TO OPEN A COCONUT

1   Make a hole in two of the three 'eyes' with a clean screwdriver or nail. Drain off and keep the liquid (coconut water) for stock.

2   Try to split the coconut in half by tapping briskly with a cleaver or hammer.
3   Scrape out the flesh using a small knife, potato peeler, or if you can get one from the Thai shop, a purpose-made coconut scraper. .
4   Pare off the dark inner skin (except on a younger coconut when it is soft and inoffensive – and always for desserts, when you need whiter flesh).

The flesh can be eaten in chunks or scrapings. It is also used to make coconut milk (not to be confused with coconut water).

TO MAKE COCONUT MILK

1   Put the scraped flesh into a bowl with warm water. Squeeze it for a few minutes. Strain it. Thais use a purpose-made two-handled close-weave basket for this job. This is called the first pressing and it creates thick coconut milk (also called coconut cream).
2   Repeat stage one twice more for the second and third pressing.

Each pressing yields a thinner result. Medium coconut milk is a mixture of the second and third pressings. Thin is the third only.

COOKING WITH COCONUT MILK

Two observations. Firstly, Thais generally add coconut milk early on in the cooking. They like to 'reduce' it (thicken it) on slow heat, with garlic or initial pastes. This has the advantage of properly mixing the fragrances, and creating a great subsequent taste.

Secondly, coconut milk sometimes appears to curdle when heat is applied. Don't worry. This is normal. It can't curdle, so just keep stirring.

READY-TO-USE COCONUT PRODUCTS

For various reasons, we may wish to use factory coconut products. There are a number:

CANNED COCONUT MILK

Available in 400ml (13fl oz) cans, this is a really excellent product. If you don't shake the can before you open it, you'll find that the top third is thick cream, underneath is thin milk. When shaken it becomes medium. Keeping the can in the fridge before opening makes the separation even better.

COCONUT MILK POWDER

The problem with using tinned coconut milk is that you are sometimes left with an excess. It can be frozen, but it's a mite inconvenient. Coconut milk powder, a relatively new product, solves this. It is a fine white powder, made by freeze-drying coconut milk. It can be used by the spoonful and keeps indefinitely in an airtight container to be used when required. Ignore any instruction on the packet which advises you to 'mix with water' before use. Simply add it to your cooking (as the recipes which use it direct) and stir it in. It won't go lumpy. Then add water to the cooking if it needs it.

Three other coconut products are:

CREAMED COCONUT

This is a 200g (7oz) block, which is a combination of freshly grated coconut flesh and coconut oil, which sets solid. It must be kept under refrigeration. To use, boil a little water. Cut off the amount required and melt it in the hot water. If you try to fry it without water, it will burn.

DESICCATED COCONUT

This is coconut flesh scrapings which are air-dried. It can be used by adding it dry to your cooking, or by simmering it in water and straining it to create coconut milk, or by lightly toasting it under the grill.

COCONUT OIL

Coconut oil comes set solid in bottles with no instructions as to how to extract it. Extraction is, however, simple. Ensure the cap is screwed on tightly, then immerse the bottle in hot water for a few minutes. The oil becomes transparent and pourable as it liquefies. It can be used instead of sunflower or soy oils in any dish which uses coconut milk or flesh.

FISH SAUCE
Nam pla

THIS IS THE product you either love or hate. My wife Dominique hates it and in blind tasting sessions she can tell if I've sneaked in even one drop. Thais (and all their neighbours) love it. So what is it? It is a clear brown liquid, the colour of beer. Different brands vary in darkness and in quality. The main area for producing fish sauce is in Rayong, near Pattaya. The favourite Thai brand (best quality) is Tipparous, which has a picture of weighing scales on it.

Fish sauce is factory made and is smelly. There are a number of 'own label' brands in the West such as Blue Dragon (and all with ill-fitting tops).

Its main ingredient is any fish (but mostly, small anchovies are used) mixed with 1 : 1 salt and enough water to make it pliable in jars, which are left uncovered in the sun for one year. As it dries, the fish ferments and more water, salt and a little sugar is added. It is then strained and the clear brown liquid is bottled and ready for use.

If all that has put you off, you may like to know that you have almost certainly consumed it and enjoyed it. It has been an ingredient in the much copied Lea & Perrins Worcestershire Sauce, from it first secret formulation (unchanged to this day) in 1837. It is only in recent times that legislation has compelled manufacturers to reveal their ingredients. Lea & Perrins had to state 'anchovies' in their list (read the label!). But is it isn't called fish sauce!

Incidentally, the concept of using fermented fish and salt is far from new. The Romans used it in their mixture called *garum*. Whether that predated Thailand's version is not known. Of course, it came up-to-date in Britain (especially in Victorian times) in the form of anchovy essence.

As to using it, unless you are Dominique, the fish taste doesn't dominate. It does supply a lot of salt to your recipe, so I have not stipulated 'salt to taste' in most of my recipes. If the fish sauce does not suit you (and true vegetarians are in that category) either omit it altogether or use soy sauce. (*page 39*). The taste will, however, be different.

SHRIMP PASTE
Kapee

Like fish sauce, *kapee* is a fundamental flavour to many if not most Thai savoury recipes. They would use a tablespoon or more (I've cut that down to a teaspoon in some recipes, and even that can be omitted – with a minor change in taste – if you don't want it).

There are shrimp paste variants in Burma (*blachan*) and Indonesia (*trasi*), where it comes in hard blocks, yellow in colour. The Thai version, (*kapee*), is softer and not as strong in flavour as those, being a paste, often browny-pink in colour.

Most *kapee* is made by mashing river prawns with salt and water. It can easily be made at home as the recipe on page 42 shows. Factory versions come in tubs or jars with a wax seal. Once opened, they should last for months without refrigeration. A very important point should be made about factory *kapee*. It should always be fried at a high temperature early on in the recipe. In the unlikely event of bacteriological contamination, the heat destroys any problem.

There is a particular version of *kapee* which incorporates a particular kind of huge water beetle, about 6 or 7cm long. For your delectation a description is on page 14.

DRIED PRAWNS

S INCE THE original Thais settled along the waterways, they became, and still are, dependent on fish and shellfish. Not only do they eat it fresh at every opportunity, they mastered the art of drying it centuries ago.

Fish are gutted and boned, spread flat, then hung up on frames to dry in the sun. Within a day of fierce Thai sunshine they are bone dry, brittle and translucent, keep indefinitely, and can be used at any time in cooking. Take a look at the Thai shop and like as not, there will be plenty of choice. Although I've not used dried fish in the recipes in this book you can use them in any wet (not fried) fish dish by reconstituting them in water first.

Likewise dried prawns. These I have specified in certain recipes. Small ones are available in large sachets. They last indefinitely, kept in an airtight jar, and are used as required.

RICE

R ICE IS THE staple food in Thailand. Full details about Thai rice appear on page 149.

NOODLES

N OODLES WERE brought to Thailand by the Chinese. They are very popular, being easy to store dried, and quick to reconstitute. Full details about Thai noodles appear on page 157.

SALT

F ISH SAUCE is intensely salted (*page 36*). It appears in virtually every savoury recipe. Consequently, I have not stated 'salt to taste' as I would normally. If you prefer to omit fish sauce then please salt to taste. Thais use rock salt.

SUGAR
Nam taan

S UGAR IS used in almost every Thai savoury recipe. The sugar they use is palm sugar (*nam taan peep*) which is processed from the Palmyra tree.
It is available from the Thai shop in packets or tins and is soft, yellowy and fudge-like. Kept in the fridge it lasts about three months. It is worth getting because it has a gorgeous flavour, unlike any other sugar, and it is very sweet. An alternative is *nam taan puck*, which is palm sugar hardened into a block. Since it is dehydrated, it is even sweeter, being concentrated, and it lasts indefinitely. Indian *jaggery* is a suitable alternative.
At the risk of upsetting my Thai friends, I have to say that I prefer to cook my savoury dishes without sugar, or at most put sugar into just one dish which goes to make up your menu selection. Consequently, I have put sugar as an optional extra in the relevant recipes.

SOY

S OYA BEANS are the Chinese answer to everything. As their supplier of protein, they have made this unremarkable and rather tasteless small round bean into something amazing. How this came about is lost in the mists of time but thousands of years ago the Chinese learned to use the soya bean.

In its natural state it is small and pale cream in colour. When fermented it turns black, brown or yellow and is then soft enough to make into thick salty flavouring pastes and thin salty runny sauce of varying strengths. The ancients learned to compress the bean into cheese-like blocks (bean curd or tofu – see below) which could be crumbled or cut, and cooked. They also learned how to make it into a cooking oil and into a milk-like drink.

Soya in various forms appears in certain Thai dishes, especially those with a Chinese influence.

SOY SAUCE

THIS MAKES occasional appearances in Thai dishes. It is made from soya beans which are fermented in vats with salt and water for months, before the brown liquid is strained off. It can be used as an alternative to fish sauce (*page 36*), though this changes the nature of the dish. There are two types of Chinese soy sauce – thin or light soy sauce is light in colour, and saltier than the dark soy sauce. This is dark brown and thicker. A third kind of soy sauce, and my favourite, comes from Indonesia. Called *katchup manis*, it is very dark, very thick, salty and sweet and is quite delicious. I refer to it as sweet soy in the recipes. *Katchup*, incidentally, means 'sauce' in Indonesian hence tomato ketchup.

TOFU

TOFU, OR BEAN curd is another Chinese import into Thailand based on the soya bean. It appears in some Thai recipes (two in this book). It has the texture of cheese. It can be either soft (*taohou* in Thai) or firm (*tao kwa*) depending on the process. It is made by soaking and puréeing white soya beans. The purée is then boiled in water which is strained to make soya milk. This is brought back to the simmer and a curdling agent, such as lemon juice, is added. It is then re-strained and the solid matter is compressed in moulds. After some time the result is a firm block of tofu. The process was used around 2,000 years ago by the scientists of an emperor of the Han dynasty (206 BC to AD221).

Tofu is easily obtained in packets from delicatessens and health-food shops. It is virtually flavourless and very high in protein. It is used for its texture and can be diced, sliced, minced or mashed then boiled, baked, stir-fried or deep-fried.

BEAN CURD SHEETS

MADE FROM soya beans, these sheets are skin-like, pale yellow, really thin and translucent, but quite tough, though care is needed in their handling. Available from oriental stores, in packets, the sheets are used as wrappers, following reconstituting in water. They can be substituted for wonton wrappers in any of my recipes.

WONTON WRAPPERS

ALSO KNOWN as wonton pastry, sheets or skin. Wonton is a type of very thin pastry made from wheat flour and egg. Invented in China, the normal size of each sheet is around 8cm square. A larger version, called spring roll wrapper, is about 30cm square.

Specialist bakers make this pastry and it takes years of training to produce translucently thin pastry of an even thickness. For this reason, it is convenient to buy ready-made wrappers. They are available at specialist shops, frozen, in packets containing varying numbers of sheets. If you cannot obtain them, filo pastry or samosa pads are good alternatives.

Whatever type of sheet you use, because they are so thin they can quickly dry out and become brittle. To prevent this, thaw the packet before opening it. Once opened, keep the wrappers covered with a cold, clean damp tea towel at all times, except when removing a sheet for use.

RHIZOMES
Ginger, Galangal, Turmeric

GINGER

Ginger is a rhizome (or root) which grows underground, and is native to Asia and other suitable climates. Although it comes in three forms (fresh, whole dried and as a powder), fresh is the best way to use it. It stays fresh for many months after being cropped. It is readily available at green-grocers. Size is not always a guide to quality. It should look plump, not withered, and have a pinky beige skin and a slight sheen. When cut, the ginger should be a primrose-cream colour with no sign at all of blue or staleness. It is not possible to tell if it is stale until you cut it, so if you know your greengrocer well, ask him to cut it before you buy it. It should not be stringy or very dry and tough.

Ginger is quite hot and pungent so do not overdo the quantity unless you are a ginger freak.

YOUNG GINGER

Also called stem ginger, this is paler and jucier than ordinary ginger, for which it can be substituted.

LESSER GINGER

Lesser ginger has a cluster of yellowy brown fingers, each averaging between 6cm to 15cm in length and 1cm in diameter, which drop down from a central stem. It has pale yellow flesh which is milder, sweeter and more aromatic than ordinary ginger. It is used in salads and light curries. Available from the Thai shop, lesser ginger keeps and is used like ordinary ginger.

GALANGAL

Galangal is pale creamy buff with tinges of flamingo pink and regular thin dark stripes around it. It has a more pointed appearance than ginger. Its flesh is white and its flavour is quite distinctive. Available from Thai and Chinese shops, it should be used whenever you can get it in Thai cooking. It is kept and used like ginger.

TURMERIC

Turmeric is also a rhyzome, and a relative of ginger. The fresh root is available in various varieties and shapes from the Thai or Indian shop. The skin is browner than ginger. The flesh is bright orange. It is used in some Thai recipes, as is the more familiar turmeric powder.

KAPEE
Shrimp Paste

Available ready-made (*page 36*) *kapee* is a virtually ubiquitous Thai ingredient. It can be made at home, relatively easily. I use a mixture of packet dried prawns and prawns in brine which comes in tubs (prawns and shrimps are one and the same). Use some of the brine (keep the rest for stock). This recipe makes a reasonable quantity. Freeze the surplus in the ice-cube mould (*page 24*).

───────── MAKES: ABOUT 300G (10½OZ) PASTE ─────────

175g (6oz) prawns
about 100ml (3½ fl oz) brine
60g (2oz) dried prawns
2 tablespoons fish sauce (*page 36*)

1   Strain the prawns and brine.
2   Put them, the measured brine, the dried prawns and the fish sauce into the blender and mulch to a fine but thick purée.
3   Use as required or freeze as described above.

NOTE: *The Thai version is purple-grey in colour because raw prawns are used. This version is pink because cooked prawns are used.*

LAPAKCHEE PRIG THAI
'Magic Paste'

In many different parts of the world you'll find a trinity of basic ingredients. In Thailand the three ingredients are garlic, coriander leaves, stem and roots, and white pepper corns (or fresh green pepper corns, if available). These are ground together to a paste and stir-fried in many a Thai dish. It is so important that Thais call it their 'magic paste'.

20 cloves garlic
200g (7 oz) fresh coriander, leaves, stems and roots.
50g (1¾oz) green or white pepper corns

1   Coarsely chop the garlic and coriander.
2   Place it in a food processor or blender and mulch to a coarse purée, using a little water if necessary.
3   The paste will keep fresh for a few days in the fridge or it can be frozen in ice cube moulds (*page 24*).

NAM GAI GAENG CHUD
Chicken Stock

Literally it means 'minimally spiced chicken water'.

Many dishes require a liquid stock base. It's worth making one or more types up in bulk and freezing them in suitable portion sizes (in large yoghurt pots, for example). Here are three types, each making enough stock for four or more dishes.

MAKES: 2 LITRES OF STOCK

2.2 litres (4 pints) water
2 skinned chicken drumsticks on the bone, left-over chicken bones, giblets, cooked meat (any amount as available)
2 tablespoons fish sauce (page 36)
4 stalks lemon grass, finely cross-cut (page 30)
50g (1¾oz) onion, chopped
2 cloves garlic, quartered

1   Bring the water to the boil in a 3.5 litre saucepan.
2   Slash the flesh on the drumsticks. Add them and the remaining ingredients to the saucepan.
3   Maintain a gentle simmer for at least 30 minutes, at most 45 minutes, stirring occasionally. Spoon off any scum.
4   Strain the liquid. Discard the solids.
5   Use as required. It will keep in the fridge for a few days, but should be re-boiled before use. It can be frozen as described on page 22.

NAM PLA GAENG CHUD
Fish Stock

Use a whole small fish (head, tail, bones and all) for best results. Alternatively, you can use filleted cod steaks enhanced with some prawns.

──────────── MAKES: 2 LITRES (4 PINTS) OF STOCK ────────────

2.2 litres (4 pints) water
1 225g-300g (8-9oz) herring
  or mackerel
2 tablespoons fish sauce
(*page 36*)

4 stalks lemon grass, finely
  cross-cut (*page 30*)
50g (1¾oz) onion, chopped
2 cloves garlic, chopped

1 Bring the water to the boil in a 3.5 litre saucepan.
2 Roughly chop up the fish, but use all of it. Add it with the remaining ingredients into the saucepan.
3 Follow the chicken stock recipe from stage 3 to the end.

NAM PAK GAENG CHUD
Vegetable Stock

A variant of the previous two stocks. True vegetarians can omit the fish sauce and replace it with light soy sauce.

──────────── MAKES: 2 LITRES OF STOCK ────────────

2.2 litres (4 pints) water
100g (3½oz) carrot
100g (3½oz) celery
50g (1¾oz) spring onions
50g (1¾oz) onion

4 stalks lemon grass, finely
  cross-cut (*page 30*)
4 cloves garlic
2 tablespoons fish sauce (*page 36*)
  or light soy

1   Bring the water to the boil in a 3.5 litre saucepan.
2   Clean and roughly chop the vegetables and the onion. Add them and the other ingredients into the saucepan.
3   Follow the chicken stock recipe from stage 3 to the end.

KRATHIAN JEOW
Crispy Fried Garlic

In this recipe garlic is very slowly fried until it goes golden brown. It can be used in cooking or as a garnish. Here are two versions – one with neat garlic, the other adding prawns. It's a big batch to save on smells and washing up which results from making numerous small batches. Freeze in an ice cube mould, then break out into freezer bags (*page 24*). See page 48 for an onion version.

─────────── MAKES: AN AMPLE QUANTITY ───────────

30 cloves garlic
100ml (3½oz) sunflower or soy oil

1   Peel then chop the garlic into thin strips.
2   Heat the oil until it nearly smokes (190°C).
3   Add the garlic. Stir-fry on low heat so that it slowly simmers but the garlic does not blacken.
4   Cook for about 10 minutes, stirring from time to time.
5   Strain off the oil. Keep it for future cooking.
6   Use the garlic as required. Freeze the surplus as described.

CORIANDER

KRATHIAM JEOW GUNG
Crispy Fried Garlic with Prawns

Use dried prawns (*page 37*) They become 'prawn flakes' – a very popular Thai garnish/condiment

MAKES: AN AMPLE QUANTITY

20 cloves garlic
100g (3½oz) dried prawns

1   Follow the previous (crispy fried garlic) recipes to the end of stage 3. About 6 minutes into stage 4, add the dried prawns and continue to the end of the recipes.

KAI TA-KHAY
Decorative Egg Net

This is literally what it says it is: a net made with interlacing strands of egg in a non-stick frying pan. It was invented by the chefs for the Thai royal family and is highly decorative, being used to wrap around minced items or to garnish dishes such as Pad Thai.

Though they look exceedingly complicated, these nets are actually quite easy to make (you'll need a little practice) and are an excellent talking point.

MAKES: 4 NETS

2 eggs
a small plastic bag
2 tablespoons sunflower or soy oil

1   Beat the egg and transfer one quarter into the plastic bag.
2   Heat the oil in a non-stick frying pan. Swirl it around then drain it from the pan to a bowl. Put the pan back on the heat, but never allow to get too hot.

3   Snip a one millimetre or smaller hole in a corner of the bag.
4   Gently squeeze the egg out of the bag at one side of the pan and run
     it along in a straight line about 12cm long, creating a 'thread'. Build
     this up until you have made a whole lot of 'threads'.
5   Now do the same at right-angles. You've now got a net. Repeat the
     whole process (giving four layers).
6   Remove the net and rest it on kitchen paper.
7   Repeat for the other three nets.

NAM MAK KAM
Tamarind Purée

A unique essential souring agent, Thai tamarind is sold in the pod and is
quite 'young'. Since this is generally unavailable in the West, use tamarind
block which is available in a 200g (7oz) rectangular packet from Asian
stores. It keeps for 18 months in this form in the cupboard. This makes a
large batch, which will keep fresh for a few days in the fridge. Freeze it
after that in the ice cube mould (*page 24*).

MAKES: ABOUT 300G (10.5OZ) PURÉE)

200g (7oz) tamarind block
water as required

1   Break up the tamarind block. Put in a saucepan, cover with water and
     bring to the simmer.
2   Mulch it about and simmer for about 30-45 minutes. Keep replacing
     the water as it reduces.
3   When you have a gorgeous deep brown liquid, strain it off, working
     the pulp through the sieve to extract as much of the liquid as possible.
4   Return the stones, stalks and skin, etc., to another saucepan with
     more water and repeat the process two or three times until you've
     extracted all the tamarind juices. Discard the solids.
5   These juices can be simmered further to reduce to a thicker
     consistency.
6   Use fresh and/or freeze as noted above.

HUA-HOM JEOW
Crispy Fried Onion

1kg (2¼ lb) red onion
200ml (6fl oz) sunflower or soy oil

1 Use a saucepan or wok for this recipe. The frying pan isn't large enough.
2 Chop the onion into 2.5cm thin strips.
3 Heat the oil until it nearly smokes (190°C).
4 Add the onion. Follow the garlic recipe on page 45 to the end. You will require longer (15-20 minutes) at stage 4.
5 You can add prawns to this, as with the garlic version. Simply follow the Krathian Jeow Gung recipe on page 46.

NOTE: *This is the onion version of the crispy garlic recipe on page 45.*

THAI BASIL

CHAPTER 2
CRISPY, FRIED, GRILLED, STUFFED ITEMS

THAI PEOPLE do not generally eat starters as a separate course in the way we do in the West. That's not to say there isn't a vast range of finger foods which ideally suit as starters. In a Thai meal a selection of these might be served with the main meal and eaten in the order of the diner's choice. The choice is varied and exciting. It is colourful in both name and appearance, and it is just as tasty as it looks.

In this chapter I have brought together a number of my favourites. Some will be very familiar from the Thai restaurant – satay, wontons, spring rolls, prawn toasts and crackers. Others may be new to you – golden thread pork, emerald chicken parcels, curry puffs, pastry cloaked prawns.

Relatively simple appetisers can be made by stuffing or filling vegetables. Ideal for this purpose are any which need no cooking, and preferably those which can be given special treatment, such as decorative carving. Cucumber, radishes, tomatoes, peppers, large chillies, avocados, small lettuce leaf cups, onion cups, even celery sticks can be stuffed. As to the stuffings, ground beef, pork or chicken, prawns, or vegetables work well. Recipes for all these follow.

The dishes from this chapter are all so good that you may find yourself composing your whole meal with starters only. And, of course, they are great items for a large buffet party.

LAAB
Ground Items

Laab is a type of ground spicy meat or chicken from north Thailand where it is often eaten raw in the way we eat steak tartare. Here I am using the concept to form the ingredient(s) for stuffings or fillings for a number of recipes in this chapter, and elsewhere.

LAAB NUA
Ground Beef

Use only good quality steak for this. It gives better, less fatty meat.

MAKES: 250G (9OZ) GROUND BEEF

250g (9oz) frying steak (rump or fillet)
4 cloves garlic, chopped
2 tablespoons fresh coriander leaves and stems
2 teaspoons very finely chopped green chilli (cayenne)
1 teaspoon finely cross-cut lemon grass (*page 30*)
1 teaspoon shrimp paste (*page 36*)
½ teaspoon salt

1   Roughly chop up the meat, removing any unwanted matter.
2   Place it and all the other ingredients into the food processor and pulse it until it becomes finely ground. It should be like a thick paste. The finer it is ground the silkier is the texture when cooked.

NOTE: *Do not overload the food processor. Grinding meat is heavy work. It is better to do it in smaller batches, then mix them together at the end.*

3   To cook. Make sure the 'paste' is well mixed together then roll into balls or squares and place them on an oven tray.
4   To cook preheat the oven to 190°C (375°F) Gas 5 into which put the oven tray.
5   Bake for about 10 minutes. Inspect and if they need a little more (cut one in half to check) bake for a few more minutes.

LAAB MOO
Ground Pork

Use pork steak (or diced lean leg) and follow the previous Ground Beef recipe in its entirety.

LAAB GAI
Ground Chicken

Use skinned chicken breast and follow the previous Ground Beef recipe in its entirety.

LAAB GUNG
Ground Prawn

Use any of the above fillings, adding chopped or mashed cooked prawns to taste.

LAAB PAK
Ground Vegetables

The principle here is quite different from the previous *laab* recipes. (Indeed this is not really *laab*, but it is a tasty vegetable filling.) I use mashed potato as the anchor.

200g (7oz) mashed potato
50g (1¾oz) cooked peas
50g (1¾oz) cooked
  sweetcorn
2 tablespoons fresh coriander
  leaves and stems
2 teaspoons very finely

chopped red chilli (cayenne)
1 teaspoon finely cross-cut
  lemon grass (*page 30*)
1 teaspoon shrimp paste
  (*page 36*)
1 teaspoon fish sauce
  (*page 36*)

1   Simply mix the ingredients together.

BAI KRUAY TOO-AY
Banana Leaf Cup

There is really no substitute for banana leaves, but they are available at Thai or Asian stores. If you can get them they're fun to use. Here they are made into cups. Banana leaf is inedible of course, so the shape of the cup is achieved by using staples. The cups are filled with any of the previous stuffings. Alternatively you can use rice or Hor Mok fish, see page 118.

———————————————— MAKES: 8 CUPS ————————————————

2 or 3 fresh banana leaves	**a 12cm saucer**
small staples	**a pencil and scissors**

1   Spread the banana leaf out. Invert the saucer on to the leaf, avoiding the main rib.
2   Mark round the saucer with a pencil . Repeat until you have 8 circles.
3   Carefully cut out the circles with scissors (a).
4   Taking one circle, fold in half (but do not crease) pinch one edge together about 2cm deep and staple it (the drawing shows the principle) (b). Repeat 180° opposite (c).
6   Open the semi-circle out to make a container. Flatten its base (d). Staple at 90° round the edge. Repeat 180° opposite (e).
7   Now staple the points in flush to the sides. Carefully flatten the base and you have a square 'cup' with 2.5cm walls and a 5cm base.
8   Repeat with the other cups.

CHEF'S TIP: *Practise this using paper until you are happy.*

9   Fill the cup with cooked rice (from Chapter 10) topped with crispy garlic or onion (*page 45/48*) or ready-bought fish flakes.

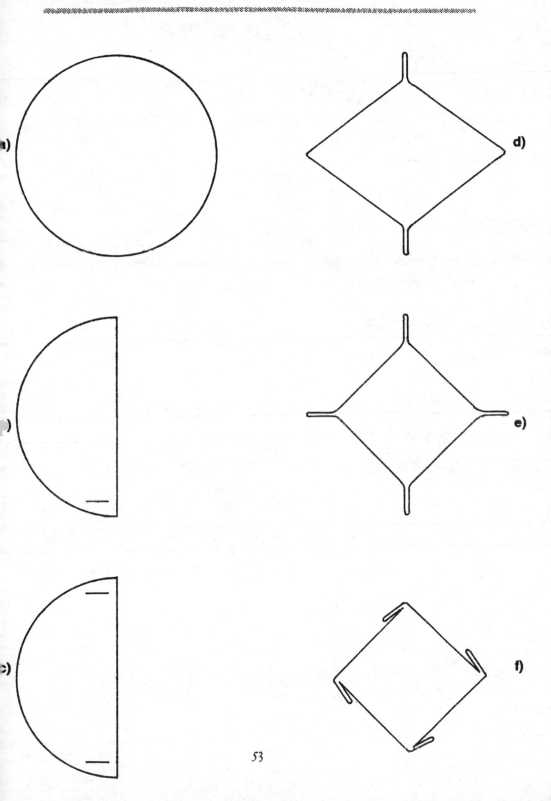

a)

d)

b)

e)

c)

f)

KAI LOOK KOEI
Son-in-Law's Eggs

The story is told at every occasion, particularly by cackling female market traders. At least, that's where I first heard it, years ago, at a Bangkok food market, translated by an effete young man, who looked more and more embarrassed at every hand gesturing cackle from the females. Eggs are a euphemism of course, and I pity the sons-in-law of those cacklers! My version uses quail eggs surrounding a hen's egg. The cacklers would have had even more fun comparing sizes.

It's a pretty dish with nearly hard-boiled eggs, deep-fried then drizzled with chilli jam (*page 170*).

———————— SERVES: 4 AS AN ACCOMPANIMENT ————————

1 large hen's egg
12 quail eggs
oil for deep-frying

chilli jam
shredded spring onion (or lime leaf)

coriander leaf for garnish

1   Par-hard-boil the hen's egg for about 10 minutes and the quail eggs for about 3 minutes, in ample water already boiling.
2   Remove the eggs from the water and run them under the cold water tap.
3   Shell them.
4   Preheat the deep-fry oil to 190°C (chip-frying temperature).
5   Carefully immerse the eggs into the oil. Deep fry until the outside of the egg goes golden (about 5 minutes).
6   Remove the eggs. Shake off excess oil and rest them on kitchen paper, then using a really sharp knife or a razor blade, halve them.
7   Place them attractively on a serving bowl. Drizzle the chilli jam over them. Garnish and serve hot.

MOO SARONG
Golden Thread Pork

These are as pretty as their name and so clever. Who thought of them? Of course, it was the chefs to the Thai royal family two centuries ago.

The idea is simple – and so they are to make. Noodles are wrapped around a filling. You can use ground pork (*laab moo page 51*) or beef, chicken or prawn.

─────────────── MAKES: 16 BALLS ───────────────

80g (3oz) dried egg noodle (or fresh, if available)
250g (9oz) raw ground pork (*page 51*)
deep fry oil

1   Soften the dried noodles (*page 161*) and select 32 long strands.
2   Divide the ground pork into 16 to make balls about 2cm in diameter.
3   Press one end of a noodle strand on to a ball to make it stick. Carefully wind it around the ball, so that the strand doesn't overlap. Use water to help it stick. With the second strand, change direction to right-angles and wind it over the original noodle. Tuck the end into the centre. The pork should be entirely covered (but if it isn't it doesn't matter).
4   Repeat with the other 15 balls (use spare noodles and/or pork for another dish).
5   Preheat the oil to 190°C (chip-frying temperature).
6   Lower the balls into the oil and fry for 3-4 minutes.
7   Remove from the fryer, shaking off the excess oil.
8   Rest them on kitchen paper.
9   Serve hot or cold.

BABY CHILLIES

GAI HOR BAI TOEY
Emerald Chicken Parcels

This delightfully named treat is another invention from the Thai royal kitchens, whose presentation is, I believe, unique. It gets its name from the packaging which is the pandanus leaf (*page 32*). This is tied around a filling, in this case marinated chicken breast, and it is then deep-fried.

As with the Banana Leaf Cup recipe (*page 52*), there is no substitute for using the pandanus leaf here, although it is available at Thai and Asian vegetable shops. It is a long thin fibrous leaf (about 50cm x 5cm).

To use the leaf for the parcel, it is cut in half longways, removing the rib.

Two knots are possible: the single and the double.

Single knot

MAKES: 8 PARCELS
---

8 pandanus leaves
8 pieces skinned raw chicken
  breast about 2.5cm square
1 teaspoon 'magic paste'
  (*page 42*)

2 teaspoons red curry paste
  (*page 137*)
1 teaspoon fish sauce
  (*page 36*)
1 tablespoon sweet soy sauce

---

1   Divide the leaves in half longways, removing the central rib, and ending up with a strip 36-40cm long and about 2.5cm wide.
2   Mix the pastes and sauces and spread them on to the chicken.
3   Hold the chicken against the leaf strip (about 5cm from one end) (a). Wrap the long end of the leaf around the chicken. Bring the long end up and round the chicken (b). Bring the long end's tip to the chicken and loop through (c). Pull the leaf's tail through (d). Bring the long end up and round again (e), with the tip to the chicken (f). Pull the tail through again tightly (g). You now have a knot with two tails encasing the chicken.
4   To cook, heat the deep-fry oil to 190°C (chip-frying temperature).
5   One by one, immerse the parcels, into the oil (too many too fast will lower the temperature too much). Fry for about 10-12 minutes (ensure the chicken is cooked right through).
6   Remove from the oil, shaking off excess oil.
7   Rest on kitchen paper.
8   Serve hot or cold.

Single leaf version

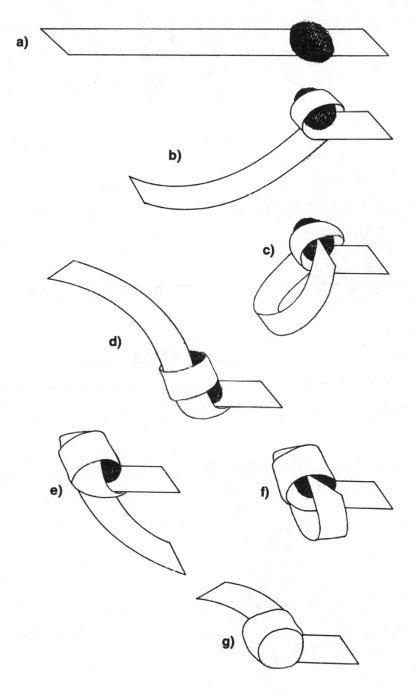

a)

b)

c)

d)

e)

f)

g)

Double leaf version

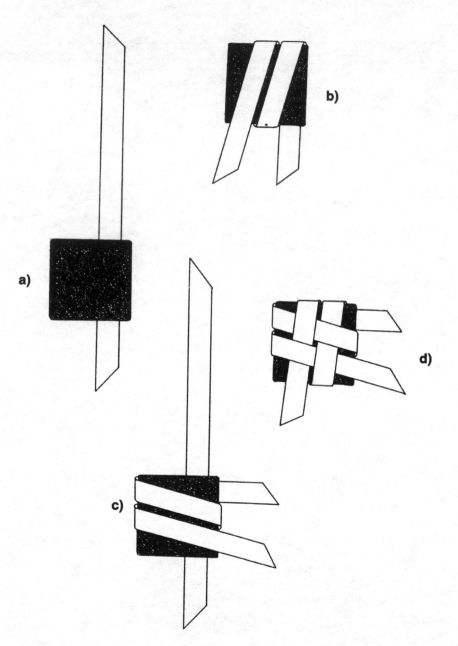

a)

b)

c)

d)

NOTE: *This knot method is not described in the text.*

SATAY GAI
Chicken Satay

Satay is one of the most popular street snacks in Bangkok. Originating in Indonesia, as beef on skewers, the story is that their name is derived from 'steak'. This word being far too much of a twister for the Oriental tongue, the word *satay* was born – and excellent it is too!

Here it is with chicken but you can use beef (best steak) or pork. It is marinated, skewered then grilled. Traditionally it is eaten with spicy peanut sauce (*page 172*).

───── MAKES: 8 SATAY SKEWERS ─────

450g to 500g (16-18oz) skinned chicken breast
8 x 20cm bamboo skewers

───── MARINADE ─────

1 tablespoons tamarind purée (*page 47*)
1 tablespoon fish sauce (*page 36*)
2 tablespoons soy sauce

2 teaspoons chilli sauce
2 tablespoons tomato ketchup
3 tablespoons ground peanuts (or fine peanut butter)

1   Cut the chicken into strips about 5cm x 2cm x 1/2cm. Since these will vary, that is just an average. Aim to get about 3 to 4 pieces per skewer (that is, 24 to 32 pieces).
2   Mix the marinade ingredients together in a large bowl. Immerse the chicken strips, cover and refrigerate for up to 60 hours.
3   Prior to cooking, soak the bamboo skewers in water for one hour. This gives them a greater resistance to burning during cooking.
4   Preheat the grill to medium heat.
5   Thread 3 or 4 pieces of chicken on to each skewer, to create a continuous run of chicken about 15cm long (leaving a little skewer poking out at each end).
6   Put the skewer on the grill rack over the grill pan. Place this in the midway position. Cook for up to 8 minutes, turning once, and checking whether the chicken is cooked right through after 5 or 6 minutes (if it isn't give it a short while more then remove).
7   Serve hot or cold.

NOTE: *A more delicate presentation can be achieved by transferring the satays from their skewer after cooking, and putting individual strips on to toothpicks.*

KARI PUB
Curry Puff

I met these on the streets of Bangkok. They are the speciality of hawkers from south Thailand. The Curry Puffs I knew before were Anglo-Indian – a kind of curry-filled Cornish pasty. The Bangkok version uses wonton wrappers (though you could use thinly rolled short or puff pastry). The filling is Thai curry. It's very spicy and makes a great snack at any time. You can freeze curry puffs before or after frying them.

MAKES: 24 CURRY PUFFS
---

24 small wonton wrappers, about 8cm to 10cm square (*page 40*)

24 teaspoons (about 110g (4oz) filling (*pages 50 to 51*)

1 tablespoon Panaeng curry paste (*page 138*)

4 tablespoons cornflour and water paste

1   Mix the filling with the curry paste.
2   Cut a circle of about 7.5cm from a wonton wrapper (a).
3   Put some filling along the centre line of the circle. (b) Paste the edges with the cornflour paste.
4   Fold over along the centre-line, and press the curved sides together to achieve a semi-circle (c).
5   Repeat with the remaining curry puffs.
6   Preheat the deep-fry oil to 190°C (chip-frying temperature).
7   Put the curry puffs into the oil one by one and fry for 8 to 10 minutes.
8   Remove them from the fryer, shaking off excess oil. Rest them on kitchen paper.
9   Serve hot or cold.

LIME LEAVES

Curry Puff (see page 61)

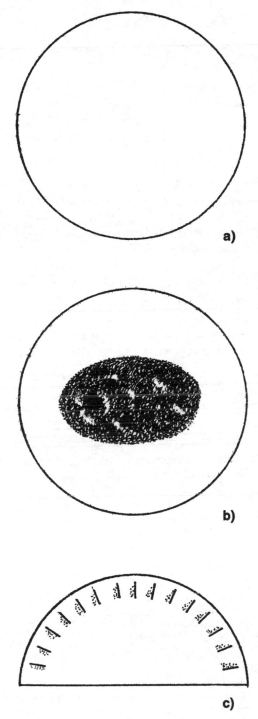

a)

b)

c)

POR PIA-TOD
Prawn Spring Roll

The celebrated Chinese Spring Roll is world class in popularity. It consists of a filling encased in thin pastry, which is wrapped into a tube shape. Thailand has its own versions. Here, using small wonton wrappers and prawn filling, is a delightful and delicate mini prawn roll.

──────── MAKES: 30 PRAWN ROLLS ────────

30 small wonton wrappers, about 8cm to 10cm square (*page 40*)

about 200g (7oz) filling (*pages 50 and 51*)

60g (2oz) beansprouts, chopped

1   Mix the filling with the beansprouts.
2   Lay one wrapper on the work surface.
3   Spread about 1 1/2 teaspoons of filling in near the top of the sheet (a).
4   Roll the top corner of the sheet over the filling (b).
5   Fold in the outside flaps (c).
6   Roll up reasonably tightly until the last corner remains (d).
7   Press this corner down with a little water. Rest the roll with this corner underneath (it helps it to stick).
8   Make the remaining prawn rolls.
9   Preheat the deep-fry oil to 190°C (chip-frying temperature).
10 One by one put about 8 rolls into the oil (too many too fast will lower the temperature too much). Fry for 5-6 minutes, until golden.
11 Remove from the fryer, shaking off the excess oil.
12 Rest on kitchen paper.
13 Cook the remaining rolls.
14 Serve hot or cold.

NOTE: *Spring rolls can be frozen before or after frying.*

FACING PAGE   An array of tempting tasties. In the black lacquer box, clockwise from top to bottom: Golden Bags, Fish Cakes, Golden Thread Pork, Emerald Chicken Parcels, Chicken Satay, Prawn Spring Rolls, Wontons, Pastry Cloaked Prawn.
Outside the box from bottom left: Rice in Banana Cup, Satay Dip, Green Curry Paste, Black Rice in Banana Cup.

Spring Roll (see page 62)

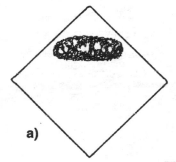

a)

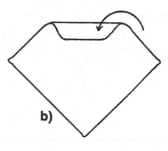

b)

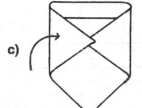

c)

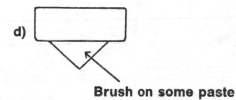

d)

Brush on some paste

KRATHAK
Pastry Cloaked Prawn

This is a fun recipe. It's simple and very effective with a secret to tell as well! It is a prawn, partly encased within a small wonton wrapper, as if it's a cloak. Its tail is exposed. It can be called Gung Hom Phah (Phah meaning 'fabric') or Pratad Lom, but if you give it a noodle tie it is called Krathak, which literally means 'fire-cracker' because it resembles a Thai firework!. Either way, the trick is to keep the prawn from curling up. The secret is an ancient one, as used in Japanese *tempura* (a technique using batter coating and deep frying): make two cuts in the prawn. (see sketch).

MAKES: 16 KRATHAKS

16 raw king prawns, about 7cm long, measured after removing the head and shell, but keeping the tail on	1 teaspoon 'magic paste' (*page 42*) 1 tablespoon fish sauce (*page 36*) 16 small wonton wrappers about 8cm square (*page 40*)

1   Wash and de-vein the prawns, keep their tails on. Then placing one on its side, cut two slits on its inside (a) or snip with a pair of scissors to prevent it curling when cooking. Repeat with the other prawns.
2   Mix the 'magic paste' with the fish sauce.
3   Marinate the prawns in this mixture for 5 to 10 minutes.
4   Place a wonton wrapper on the work top. Fold over one end (b).
5   Place a prawn, slits down, on the wrapper, with the tail projecting out from the folded end (c).
6   Fold the top corner of the wrapper over the top of the prawn (d).
7   Fold one side over the prawn (e) and fold the other side over the prawn, to create a tightly folded roll (f).
8   Tie a noodle bow (optional) (g).
9   Repeat with the other prawns.
10   Preheat the deep-fry oil to 190°C (chip-frying temperature).
11   One at a time, put 8 prawns into the oil (too many at once will reduce the temperature too fast).
12.   Fry for 8 to 10 minutes, until the prawns are cooked.
13   Remove from the fryer, shaking off the excess oil.
14   Rest on kitchen paper.
15   Repeat with the remaining prawns.
16   Serve hot with chilli sauce.

NOTE: *These can be frozen before or after frying.*

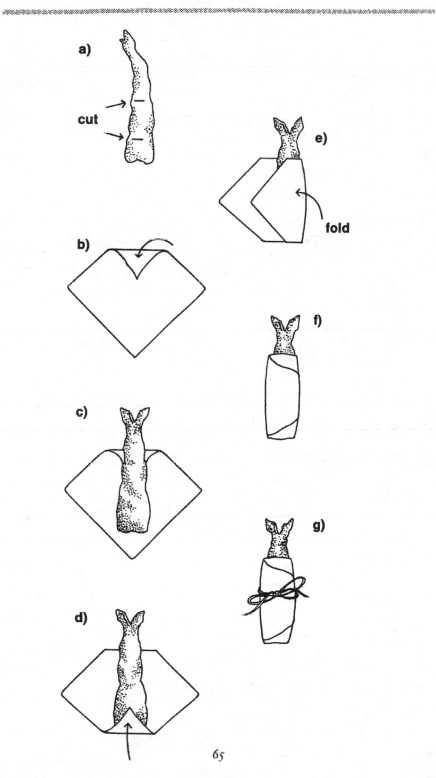

a)

cut

b)

c)

d)

e)

fold

f)

g)

65

TUNG TONG
Fried Filled Golden Bags

Tung Tong is loose 'pastry' enclosing a filling. It is based on a Chinese import, the wonton or treasure bag, and it is a popular snack. The treasure (the filling) can be pork or beef, chicken or prawn, or indeed a mixture and it is enclosed in wonton wrappers.

———————————— MAKES: 24 BAGS ————————————

24 small wonton wrappers about 12cm square (*page 40*)
24 teaspoons (about 110g (4oz)) filling (*page 50*)

1   Put a teaspoon of filling into the centre of the square.
2   Gather the points together to make an enclosed bag. Wet the top and press together to seal.
3   Press the bag down on the work surface to make a flat base.
4   Repeat with the remaining wontons. Take a pair of scissors and trim off the excess wonton wrapper to get a neat 'brush-like' effect.
5   Pre heat the deep-fry oil to 190°C (chip-frying temperature).
6   Put the wontons into the oil one by one, and fry for 8 to 10 minutes.
7   Remove and rest them on kitchen paper.
8   Serve hot.

VARIATION

WONTON CHEEN
Chinese Fried Dumplings

The main difference between these and Tung Tong is size. Wonton Cheen are much smaller and less frilly than Tung Tong. Simply follow the previous recipe, using wonton wrappers about 8cm square. The filling is correspondingly smaller. Wrap it creating less of a 'frill', then tidy up with scissors, so that the Wonton Cheen's top is almost shorn. Deep fry them, dollop some Chilli with Shrimp Paste (Nam Prig Kapi see *page 169*) on top.

NOTE: *Wonton Cheen can be steamed as an alternative to deep-frying.*

TOD MAN PLA
Fish Cake

VARIATION: Tod Man Gung
prawn cake

These are small (4cm diameter) discs deep-fried to golden and eaten hot or cold. They traditionally contain beans (the hard-to-get Thai wing beans, *tua pu*) but we can substitute that with Kenyan beans, mangetout or snow peas.

———————— MAKES: 24 FISH CAKES ————————

500g (18oz) cod fillet	very finely chopped
2 tablespoons 'magic paste' (*page 42*)	2 lime leaves, shredded (optional)
	2 tablespoons chopped fresh basil
1 tablespoon red curry paste (*page 137*)	leaves
	1 teaspoon fish sauce (*page 36*)
1 or 2 fresh Kenyan beans,	plain flour

1 Mash all the ingredients together to achieve a cohesive paste. Use a little water to achieve this as needed.
2 Quarter the mixture, then divide each quarter into 6 to achieve 24 equal size dollops.
3 Shape each dollop into a ball. Sprinkle some flour on to the work surface, then press the ball flat to achieve a disc about 4cm in diameter.
4 Preheat the deep-fry oil to 190°C (chip-frying temperature).
5 One by one place 8 fish cakes into the oil (too many will cause the oil temperature to drop too fast).
6 Fry for 6 to 8 minutes.
7 Remove and rest on kitchen paper.
8 Serve hot or cold with sauces.

NOTE: *They can be frozen before or after frying. For the prawn variation, add chopped cooked prawns to taste to the cod fillet.*

PAK TOD
Vegetable Fritters

These are the Thai equivalent of the Indian *pakora* or *bhaji* or Japanese *tempura*. They are fresh batter-coated deep-fried vegetables. Done correctly, as in this recipe, they are light and crisp and devoid of oil. The secrets are correct frying temperature and eating the fritters within minutes of cooking.

Any fresh dry vegetables will do. Make your choice from cauliflower or broccoli florets, chillies, beans, mangetout, aubergine, mushroom, carrot, onion, spring onion, celery and courgette. Since all these vegetables vary in density, I'm not giving a weight for them below. Make your selection by eye (how much will everyone eat). You can, of course, use just one vegetable, or you can 'mix-and-match' to your taste. It's up to you for this fun-and-easy dish.

SERVES: 4 AS A SNACK OR STARTER

THE BATTER

80g (3oz) cornflour (about a cupful)
2 tablespoons coconut milk powder
1 tablespoon red curry paste

2 teaspoons fish sauce (*page 36*)
2 or so cupfuls of raw vegetables, of your choice, washed, dried, prepared and cut into bite-size pieces.

1 Mix together the batter ingredients in a large bowl, using just enough water to achieve a thick pourable batter. Leave it to stand for 10 to 15 minute to 'absorb' all dryness.
2 Preheat the deep-fry oil to 190°C (chip-frying temperature).
3 Put all the vegetables into the bowl ensuring they are well coated with batter.
4 One by one, place about half the coated items into the fryer (too much too fast will lower the oil temperature too quickly). Fry for 8 to 10 minutes, or until golden, turning once or twice.
5 Remove from the fryer, shaking off the excess oil.
6 Rest on kitchen paper.
7 Repeat with the second batch.
8 Serve very hot and fresh with dips and sauces from Chapter 12.

NOTE: *Does not freeze.*

KANOM-PANG MOO GUNG
Prawn Toast

This ever-popular concept is universally found at the Chinese restaurant. Ground prawn is spread on a small piece of sliced bread and deep-fried. Not surprisingly it has made the transition not only to Thai restaurants but to the Thai street trading hawkers.

The sliced bread gives the clue that this is a Western invention. But in my view it works even better with Thai flavours.

MAKES: 16 TOASTS
---

4 slices white bread, crusts removed
100g (3½oz) prawn filling (*pages 50 to 51*)
1 tablespoon 'magic paste' (*page 42*)

1 teaspoon fish sauce (*page 36*)
1 tablespoon fresh chopped spring onions, leaves and bulbs
2 teaspoons white sesame seeds

1   Cut the crusts off the bread.
2   Mix the filling, paste, fish sauce and onion together.
3   Spread this evenly over the four slices, pressing in the seame seeds.
4   Quarter the slices.
5   Preheat the deep-fry oil to 190°C (chip-frying temperature).
6   Place 8 toasts into the deep-fryer one at a time (too many too fast will lower the oil temperature too much).
7   Fry for 5 to 6 minutes, turning a couple of times.
8   Remove from the fryer, shaking off excess oil.
9   Rest them on kitchen paper.
10 Repeat with the second batch.
11 Serve hot with dips and sauces from Chapter 12.

NOTE: *These items do not freeze very well.*

KANOM-PANG GRAWP
Crackers

Everyone surely knows and adores prawn crackers. Very much a Chinese restaurant invention, they are made from rice flour impregnated with prawn flavouring. Less known are Indonesian huge prawn crackers (called *kroepruk*). The cracker has reached Thailand, although it is quite a new concept there.

Crackers come ready to deep-fry (they are virtually impossible to make at home) in factory produced packets. Manufacturers like the worldwide Blue Dragon range sell three types: Prawn Crackers, Chiang Mia Crackers (made from pumpkin flour), and Phuket Crackers (made from cassava flour).

Crackers quickly go stale after you cook them and it's easy to make too many. To overcome this, decide before you start how many you can eat (remembering they puff up to double size).

--- TO COOK: AS MANY CRACKERS A YOU WISH TO EAT ---

crackers
deep-fry oil

1   Preheat the deep-fryer to 190°C (chip-frying temperature).
2   Add a few crackers at a time. They puff up at once.
3   Remove them with tongs or a slotted spoon, shaking off excess oil and rest on kitchen paper.
4   Repeat until all are cooked.
5   Leave them for at least 15 minutes, during which time they will become crisper.

KHAO TAANG
Rice Crispy Chips

These are Thai crispy crackers or 'chips'. Rice is cooked and pressed into a thin layer. It is then baked or fried to become crispy, and sold in bite-size pieces, either sweetened or salty. They are available at Thai food shops.

CHAPTER THREE
SOUPS

SOUPS ARE fundamental to a Thai meal. In fact, they are integral too, being served not as a starter, but as part of the main course. Actually, they do make good starters, and it is quite acceptable to serve one soup as a starter, and another, quite different soup during the main course. There are three kinds of Thai soup:

Tom Yam is the most famous. Literally meaning 'boiled salad', it should be quite chilli hot, served with your choice of chicken, meat, seafood, vegetables, or any combination. A popular presentation is the steamboat. This is a table-mounted stove with its coals under a cooking tray through which runs a central 'chimney'. The water or stock boils in the tray as the diners select their own raw ingredients, put them into the tray and let them cook at the table.

Gaeng Chud is a Chinese-influenced mildly spiced soup, containing meat and/or vegetables and, traditionally, coriander root. It is usually strained and served as a consommé.

Khao Tom is a thick soup with rice and meat or poultry. Its flavouring includes fish sauce (*nam pla*) chillies and tamarind or vinegar for a sour taste. Its spiciness varies.

TOM YAM TALAY
Thai Seafood Soup

Encapsulating all those flavours which are so essentially Thai, this mixed seafood soup is light and entrancing, fragrant yet tongue-tinglingly sour, salty and light sweet, herby and – oh, it's just fantastic – you'll just have to try it for yourself! Tom Yam is one of Thailand's national dishes.

--- SERVES: 4 ---

about 250g (9oz) mixed raw
  seafood of your choice (king
  prawns, fish chunks, small
  prawns, crab legs, squid,
  mussels, etc.)
about 700ml (1¼ pints) fish
  stock (*page 44*)
1 tablespoon magic paste
  (*page 42*)

1 teaspoon shrimp paste
  (*page 36*)
2 tablespoons tinned sweetcorn or baby corn
3 or 4 dried or fresh lime
  leaves (if available)
1 stalk lemon grass, cut to a
  tassel (*page 30*)
juice of 1 lime

--- GARNISH ---

**some whole coriander leaves
3 or 4 red chillies**

1 Prepare the mixed seafood by divesting it of unwanted matter, and washing it, then cutting it as you wish.
2 Bring the fish stock to the boil in a 2.25 litre saucepan (or larger). Add the seafood and all the other ingredients except the garnish.
3 Simmer literally until the seafood becomes cooked (which will be between 5 and 12 minutes depending on the size of the seafood pieces).
4 Place into serving bowls and garnish.

VARIATIONS

Tom Yam has many variations which get their name from the principal ingredient.

TOM YAM GAI
Thai Chicken Soup

Use 250g (9oz) of skinned filleted chicken breast, cut into thin strips, in place of the seafood. The remaining ingredients and method remain the same.

TOM YAM NUA
Thai Beef Soup

Use 250g (9oz) of lean fillet steak, cut into thin strips, in place of the seafood. The remaining ingredients and method remain the same.

TOM YAM MOO
Thai Pork Soup

Use 250g (9oz) of lean pork, cut into thin strips, in place of the seafood. The remaining ingredients and method remain the same.

TOM YAM GUNG
Thai Prawn Soup

As beef, but use whole raw king prawns.

GALANGA

TOM YAM GAI NAM KATEE
Chicken Soup with Coconut Milk

This version is much richer than standard Tom Yam because of its coconut milk.

———————————— SERVES: 4 ————————————

150g (5½oz) skinned chicken breast, cut into strips

1 tablespoon sunflower or soya oil

3 cloves garlic, finely chopped

200ml (7 fl oz) thick coconut milk

1 lemon grass stalk cut to a tassel (*page 30*)

1 red cayenne chilli, shredded

3 lime leaves, shredded (if available)

about 700ml (1¼ pints) chicken stock (*page 43*)

1 teaspoon tamarind purée (*page 47*)

1 teaspoon brown sugar

1 teaspoon ground white pepper

2 tablespoons chopped spring onion leaves

3 tablespoons very finely chopped basil leaves

fish sauce to taste (*page 36*)

freshly squeezed lime juice to taste

some coriander leaves to garnish

1 Heat the oil in a 2.25 litre saucepan. Stir-fry the garlic for 30 seconds. Add the coconut milk and bring to the simmer.

2 Add the lemon grass, chilli and lime leaves and stir for a couple of minutes.

3 Add the chicken strips and continue stirring for about 3 minutes.

4 Add the stock, tamarind purée, sugar and pepper and simmer for a final 8 to 10 minutes.

5 Add the spring onion and basil leaves. Season with fish sauce and lime juice. Serve hot.

KHAO TOM KAI
Rice Soup with Egg

As we have seen, rice is very highly regarded by Thai people, so much so that 'let's eat' translates literally to 'eat rice'. This rice soup is regarded as one of the best ways to 'eat rice'. It is taken at breakfast, as a snack, at lunch or dinner. It is given to the fit, the sick and the hung-over, from babes to the elderly – in fact it's take anytime, by anyone as a cure-all. It can be strained as a consommé, but it is usually not, being quite thick (depending on how much rice is used). Spicing varies the taste (or depending on its exact purpose) from bland to pungent, the latter being more likely for 'the morning after'!

Like Tom Yam, Khao Tom can be enjoyed with mixed seafood, prawns, chicken, beef, pork or vegetables. Here it is with egg. For a thicker soup, double the rice quantity.

***

SERVES: 4

***

75g (2¾oz) jasmine or long grained rice

700ml (1¼ pints) chicken stock

1 tablespoon magic paste (*page 42*)

1 teaspoon shrimp paste (*page 36*)

1 teaspoon chilli jam (*page 170*)

1 lemon grass stalk, cut to a tassel (*page 30*)

2.5cm cube of ginger, shredded

2 chicken or duck eggs

2 tablespoons chopped spring onion leaves

2 tablespoons chopped basil leaves

1 to 3 red chillies, chopped

fish sauce to taste

***

1   Immerse the rice in ample cold water for about 10 minutes.

2   During this time bring the stock to the simmer in a 2.25 litre saucepan. Add the pastes, chilli jam, lemon grass, and ginger.

3   Rinse the rice several times, until the water runs more or less clear.

4   Add the rice to the soup. Stir until it is swirling around (to prevent it sticking to the bottom of the pan).

5   Simmer for about 10 minutes.

6   Put the eggs into the soup and as the yolks start to set, break them, but don't whisk or stir vigorously. Simmer until the rice is completely tender.

7   Add the leaves and chillies and season with the fish sauce, then serve hot.

PAK GAENG-CHUD
Mildly Spiced Vegetable Consommé

The Thai call this soup mild, but I've met this as pungently chillied (with *nam prig*) as you could wish. So I've included this joy as an option. It must be strained and served as a consommé, with, at most, a few pieces of 'something' to give it interest (here it's noodles), plus, of course, garnish.

SERVES: 4

900ml (1½ pints) water
50g (1¾oz) spring onion
50g (1¾oz)carrot, shredded
60g (2oz)baby sweetcorn, sliced
30g (1oz)aubergine, chopped
1 to 3 tablespoons *nam prig* – optional (*page 168*)
2 teaspoons 'magic' paste (*page 42*)

1 teaspoon tamarind purée
1 tablespoon chopped red pepper
1 tablespoon chopped green pepper
2 stalks lemon grass, finely cross-cut (*page 30*)
1 tablespoon chopped basil leaf
3 lime leaves, shredded (if available)
50g (1¾oz)spring onion leaves

light soy or fish sauce

GARNISH

**a few dried egg noodles
some whole coriander leaves
red chilli tassels**

1 Bring the water to the simmer in a 3.5 litre saucepan.
2 Chop the spring onions, separating the bulbs from the leaves.
3 Add the onion bulbs, carrot, baby corn, aubergine, *nam prig*, garlic, tamarind, pepper and the lemon grass.
4 Simmer for about 10 minutes.
5 Add the leaves (including the spring onion leaves). Simmer for a further minute. Strain and discard the solids (keep a few bits for serving).
6 Season with soy or fish sauce to taste. Add the noodles. Remove the pan from the stove and leave it for a few minutes to allow the noodles to soften.
7 Serve into soup bowls and garnish.

PED GAENG-CHUD MANAO DONG
Duck Consommé with Vinegared Lime

Duck is very popular in Thailand and is prolifically bred in the farms and waterways all over the country. In this recipe an entire duck (skin, bones and all) would be used. Here, I prefer to discard the fatty skin and to use the leg, with bone. At a higher cost, you could use one filleted breast. This recipe is inspired by Bangkok's Oriental Hotel.

SERVES: 4

500g (18oz) duck drumstick and thigh, weighed after skinning
700 (1¼ pints) chicken stock (*page 43*)
2 teaspoon magic paste (*page 42*)

4 dried cloud-ear mushrooms
1 pickled lime, finely chopped (*page 173*)
1 tablespoon brine from the lime
1 teaspoon *nam prig* (*page 168*)
6 fresh basil leaves, shredded
sweet soy sauce

1   Separate the duck drumsticks from the thighs. Slash the flesh.
2   Bring the stock to the simmer in a 3.5 litre saucepan.
3   Add the duck, and everything except the basil and the soy. Simmer for 20 minutes.
4   Add the basil. Season to taste with the soy sauce. Simmer for a few more minutes.
5   Serve with the duck still on the bone.

AUBERGINE

GAENG-PHET NUA GUB WUN-SEE

Beef And Noodle Curry Soup

Beef noodle soup is one of the most popular street hawker dishes. There are as many versions as traders — some use minced beef, others (as here) strips. Some use vermicelli noodles, others wide-rice noodles. Here I'm using *wun-see* glass noodles. I'm also incorporating curry paste for a really super taste.

SERVES: 4

200g (7oz) lean sirloin steak
50g (1¾oz)glass (cellophane) noodles *wun-see*
700ml (1¼ pints) chicken stock
2 tablespoons sunflower or soy oil

3 cloves garlic, sliced
2cm cube of ginger, shredded
1½ tablespoons curry paste, any type (*pages 136 to 139*)
2 tablespoons chopped coriander leaves
2 teaspoons *nam prig* (*page 168*)

fish sauce (*nam pla*) to taste

GARNISH

---

some crispy noodles (*page 164*)
some fresh basil leaves

---

1   Divest the steak of unwanted matter and cut the meat into thin strips.
2   Soak the noodles for exactly 20 minutes in warm water.
3   Meanwhile, bring the stock to the simmer in a 3.5 litre saucepan.
4   In your wok, heat the oil, stir-fry the garlic, ginger and curry paste for a minute or so.
5   Add the beef strips and briskly stir-fry for about 4 minutes turning frequently.
6   Add the (strained) noodles to the saucepan and the fried beef, plus the leaves and *nam prig*.
7   Simmer briefly (or the noodles will enlarge too much). Season to taste with the fish sauce.
8   Serve at once, garnished with crispy noodles (if available) and basil leaves.

CHAPTER 4
SALADS

There is no salad like a Thai salad. In fact, the only resemblance with everyone else's salad is that it is served cold. Called *yam*, (pronounced 'yum'), the Thai salad is virtually a meal on its own, and a very fragrant and spicy one at that. I can't resist saying 'yum yum' because that's what one should say when one tastes it.

Thai salad should maintain a good balance between salty and sour, and whilst not being obvious, it should have a slightly sweet after taste. In Thailand it would never be served as a meal on its own or even as a course. It is always part of a meal – and a very important part. That's not to say that you cannot have one of these salads unaccompanied. Try one on a hot summer's day with a glass of bubbly!

Here are seven astonishingly varied Thai salads, and a rather special coconut salad dressing, which can accompany any of the salads if you wish. Two more salads, one rice, one noodle, appear on pages 156 and 162.

PLA NUA YAANG GUB AA-NGOON
Salad of Stir-fried Beef with Grapes

I was given this recipe by Sarnsern Gajaseni, an articulate teacher, passionate about Thai food. While he 'knocked' this dish up for me in less than ten minutes, he explained that odd numbers are lucky in Thailand, (hence seven chillies), that seedless grapes cost a day's wages for a half kilo in Bangkok and, in his charming sing-song Thai accent, he explained that the translation of *Pla Nua Yaang Gub Aa-ngoon* is far more picturesque than 'beef and grape salad'. It literally means: 'a kind of spicy salad of beef grilled, with grapes'. It is picturesque, too. And it is very tasty. Take 10 minutes to find out!

SERVES: 4

250g (9oz) lean fillet steak, weighed after stage 1

3 tablespoons sunflower or soy oil

7 tiny Thai red bird's eye chillies (*prig kee noo*) or 1 Indian red cayenne (chilli)

1 teaspoon 'magic paste' (*page 42*)

1 teaspoon palm sugar (or brown sugar)

2 lemon grass stalks, finely cut cross-ways (*page 30*)

3 or 4 lime leaves, shredded

20 black and/or white seedless grapes, halved

GARNISH

some curly lettuce leaves
some whole mint leaves
red chilli tassel

1 Divest the steak of any unwanted matter. Cut it into thin strips, about 4cm x 2cm x 4mm each.

2 Heat the oil in your wok. Add the chillies (whole) and paste and stir-fry for 30 seconds. Add the meat strips, sugar, most of the lemon grass and lime leaves, and briskly stir-fry for about 3 minutes, turning from time to time. You are trying to achieve a meat colour just browner than pink, for maximum tenderness.

3 Transfer the meat and liquid from the pan to a mixing bowl to stop the cooking.

4 When it is cold, add the grapes, and toss well.

5   On the serving plate, arrange the curly lettuce then place the salad on to it.

6   Garnish with the remaining lemon grass and lime leaf along with the mint leaves, and chilli tassel.

CHEF'S TIP: *To cut thin strips of meat, chill the steak in the freezer for about 45 minutes. It is then hard but not frozen and it will cut easily.*

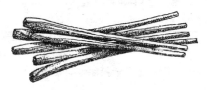

LEMON GRASS

PLA NANG MOO ISSAN
Pork Salad

Shangri-La is the place of one's dreams. Bangkok's Shangri-La Hotel's dinner buffet is aptly named. It is staged (yes, that's the word for it is theatre) every night on their expansive open-air terrace, beside the river Chao Praya. A million white pea lights adorn the trees and trellises. A team of chefs (dozens of them) in gleaming whites arrive in procession with their feasts of dishes, which they lay out in decorative order in a number of pavilions and a central table from which the diners select their fill.

I can safely say it's the best buffet I've ever had. This salad from northern Thailand is one dish which regularly appears. It uses minced pork, but its outstanding subtlety is the use of pork rind, so soft and delicately cooked that you'd believe it to be translucent thin noodle strips.

SERVES: 4

150g (5½oz) minced lean pork
6 pieces bacon with rind
500ml (18 fl oz) water
2 lemon grass stalks, cut long-wise into tassels (*page 30*)
2 tablespoons sunflower or soya oil
1 stalk lemon grass, cross-cut (*page 30*)
3 or 4 lime leaves (if available)

shredded
1 or 2 red chillies, sliced
1 teaspoon fish sauce (*page 36*)
1 tablespoon chopped purple basil leaves
2 tablespoons chopped radiccio leaves
50g (1¾oz) beansprouts
4 very finely chopped spring onions, leaves and bulbs

GARNISH

some radiccio leaves
basil leaves

---

1   Cut the rinds off the bacon and snip into 4cm lengths. Keep the bacon for some other use.

2   Bring a half litre (18 fl oz) of water to the simmer. Add the rinds, and the lemon grass stalks cut longways. Simmer for 20 minutes.

3   Add the minced pork and simmer for 10 minutes more. Strain, keeping the water, now a rich flavoured stock.

4   Heat the oil in your wok. Add the minced pork, and rinds, cross-cut lemon grass, lime leaves, red chillies and fish sauce and stir-fry for about 10 minutes. Add in about 100ml (3½ fl oz) of the stock little by little. Keep the rest for another use. Take the pan off the heat.

5   When it is cold, add the remaining ingredients and garnish.

YAM TALAI
Seafood Salad

I expect by now you agree with me that the Thais have wonderful seafood recipes. Yam Talai seafood salad is their king of salads. And to emphasize the point, my version here uses king prawns as well as small prawns, squid, mussels and cod.

SERVES: 4

8 king prawns, shelled
300g (10½oz) small prawns
8 squid rings
12 mussels out of shell
150g (5½oz) cod steaks, chopped
200ml (6 fl oz) water
2 lemon grass tassels (*page 30*)
2 tablespoons sunflower or soya oil
1 teaspoon shrimp paste (*page 36*)
1 clove garlic, chopped

2 stalks lemon grass, finely cross-cut (*page 30*)
3 lime leaves, shredded (if available)
1 red chilli, sliced
1 tablespoon sliced fresh green bell pepper
3 or 4 spring onion leaves and bulbs
1 tablespoon very finely chopped coriander leaves
1 teaspoon fish sauce ((*page 36*)
some fresh beansprouts

GARNISH

1   Heat the water in a saucepan. Add the lemon grass tassels and the seafood. Simmer for about 4 or 5 minutes. Strain, keeping the water (now a stock) for later.
2   Heat the oil in your wok. Add the shrimp paste and garlic and briskly stir for 30 seconds. Add the seafood, cross-cut lemon grass, lime leaves, red chilli, green pepper and spring onions and stir-fry this mixture for about 3 minutes.
3   Add the coriander leaves and fish sauce, stir-fry for a few seconds.
4   Allow to cool. Garnish with fresh beansprouts.

YAM GAI TUA-PU
Chicken and Bean Salad

This is a very pleasant salad. Tua-pu are winged beans, rather strange in shape, which are sometimes available at Thai grocers. A suitable substitute is mangetout or snowpeas. But there's more to this recipe than its name suggests. It has coconut milk which makes it really creamy, and it also has toasted peanuts.

──────────── SERVES: 4 ────────────

200ml (7 fl oz) coconut milk
250g (9oz) chicken breast, skinned and chopped into thin shreds about 3cm x 3mm x 3mm
2 stalks lemon grass, crosscut (*page 30*)
1 teaspoon fish sauce (*page 36*)
3 or 4 lime leaves, shredded (if available)

200g (7oz) winged beans or Kenyan beans or mangetout, sliced
1 red cayenne chilli, shredded
1 teaspoon palm or brown sugar (optional)
3 or 4 spring onions, bulbs and leaves
2 tablespoons chopped basil leaves
50g (1¾oz) peanuts, toasted and chopped

──────────── GARNISH ────────────

some lettuce leaves
some green cayenne chilli, chopped
some toasted desiccated

coconut (*page 35*)
hard-boiled egg, crumbled
some chilli jam to drizzle on (*page 170*)

1   Bring the coconut milk to the simmer in your wok.
2   Add the chicken, lemon grass, fish sauce and lime leaves and simmer gently for 5 minutes, stirring occasionally.
3   Add the beans or mangetout, chilli, sugar and continue to stir-fry for about 5 minutes.
4   Add the spring onions, basil leaves and the peanuts. Stir in and when sizzling, remove the wok from the heat.
5   When cold, put it into a serving bowl on a bed of lettuce, then garnish.

YAM NAW MIA FARANG
Asparagus Salad

This salad uses fresh asparagus, a very popular seasonal Thai vegetable. It is really simple to make using minimal ingredients.

———— SERVES: 4 AS AN ACCOMPANIMENT OR STARTER ————

350g (12oz) fresh asparagus, weighed after stage 1	1 or 2 red cayenne chillies, chopped
3 tablespoons sunflower or soya oil	1 teaspoon sesame seeds
3cm cube of ginger or galangal, shredded	1 teaspoon fish sauce (*page 36*)
	1 teaspoon sweet soy sauce

———— GARNISH ————

whole coriander leaves	lime wedges
shredded spring onion leaves	some chilli jam to drizzle on (*page 170*)

1   Wash the asparagus and cut off the stalks from the point where they get pithy.
2   Steam them briefly to soften (or microwave).
3   Heat the oil in the wok and stir-fry the ginger, chillies, and sesame seeds for about a minute.
4   Add the asparagus and stir-fry for a further 2 or 3 minutes.
5   When cold, add the fish and soy sauces, garnish and serve at once.

YAM YAI
'Large' Vegetable Salad

Concise in its description, as ever, this literally means 'large' salad. Large in this context means a wide mixture of ingredients, the bulk of which are vegetables. There is no limit to which vegetables you can use, and in what combination. Here is my example. Thais would generally add some kind of cooked meat and shrimps. I've given an option here (which I met in Thailand), using duck egg and duck liver, which can be omitted if you prefer.

6 tablespoons sunflower or
soya oil
2 cloves garlic, sliced
3cm cube of ginger, shredded
1 tablespoon cross-cut lemon
grass (*page 30*)
80g (3oz) duck liver (optional) cut into strips, 4cm x
5mm x 5mm
1 teaspoon fish sauce
(*page 36*)
2 teaspoons sweet soy sauce
1 tablespoon tomato ketchup
1 teaspoon palm or brown
sugar (optional)
1 or more red chillies,
cross-cut

2 tablespoons rice vinegar
100g (3½oz) celery, chopped
2 tablespoons chopped red bell
pepper
6cm cucumber, cut into small
cubes
4 or 5 spring onions, bulbs and
leaves
100g (3½oz) beansprouts
1 large carrot, shredded
6 cherry tomatoes, quartered
50g (1¾oz) button mushrooms,
chopped
6 to 8 spinach leaves, chopped
1 tablespoon very finely chopped
coriander leaves
2 tablespoons chopped basil leaf

GARNISH

1 duck egg hard-boiled and
chopped (optional)
some toasted peanuts

some chopped chives or garlic chives
toasted desiccated coconut
(*page 35*)

1 Heat the oil in your wok. Stir-fry the garlic and ginger for 20 seconds.
   Add the lemon grass and liver and briskly stir-fry for a couple of
   minutes.
2 Take the wok off the heat and add the fish and soy sauces, the ketchup,
   sugar, chilli and vinegar mixing in well. Allow to cool.
3 Mix the vegetables and leaves, and the above mixture together. Test
   for seasoning, adding more fish sauce if needed.
4 Place the lettuce leaves as a bed on your serving dish then carefully
   arrange the salad on top. Garnish and serve.

NOTE: *The coconut dressing on page 88 goes particularly well with this recipe.*

YAM PHONLAMAI
Savoury Fruit and Winged Bean Salad

No cooking needed for this one. I love its sweet and savoury contrasts and so do the Thais. You can choose any fruit but my personal preference (as in this recipe) is to be sure to have a mixture of citrus fruits, plus melon plus strawberries and/or raspberries. More often than not Thais would add prawns or shredded chicken, but I prefer not to. You can do that in another dish, thus maintaining a uniqueness in this salad.

SERVES: 4

4 tablespoons sunflower or soy oil

2 teaspoons fish sauce (*page 36*)

1 teaspoon palm or brown sugar

1 tablespoon very finely cross-cut lemon grass (*page 30*)

1 or more green chillies, chopped

1 clove garlic, very finely chopped

4 chopped spring onion leaves only

2 tablespoons very finely

chopped purple basil leaves

1 tablespoon very finely chopped coriander leaves

8 lime segments, all pith removed

8 orange segments, all pith removed

8 grapefruit segments, all pith removed

12 strawberries, quartered

16 raspberries, whole

1 small honeydew melon, in bite-sized pieces

16 seedless black grapes, halved

200g (7oz) water melon in bite-sized pieces

some crisp lettuce leaves or radiccio

GARNISH

some cut mint leaves
some shredded lime leaves

---

1 Mix the oil, fish sauce, sugar, lemon grass, chilli and garlic together and chill in the fridge.
2 Just prior to serving wash and prepare the fruit.
3 Mix with the dressing in a large bowl.
4 Arrange the lettuce leaves on the serving dish. Arrange the salad carefully on the leaves. Garnish and serve.

NOTE: *The coconut dressing, over, is epecially good with this salad.*

YAM AUS MAPRAO
Thai Coconut Salad Dressing

This dressing requires thin coconut milk. The third pressing or the thinnest liquid from the can (*see page 35*) is what you need, otherwise the dressing becomes too rich. It will keep in the fridge for a few days (or it can freeze). Use with salad as with French dressing.

MAKES: 275ML (10 FL OZ) DRESSING

150ml (¼ pint) thin coconut milk
50ml (2 fl oz) rice vinegar
2 to 4 tablespoons chilli jam (*page 170*)

1 teaspoon ground white pepper
2 tablespoons freshly squeezed lime juice
2 teaspoons fish sauce (*page 36*)
1 teaspoon palm or brown sugar

1   Simply mix everything together, chill and serve.

PEPPER ON VINE

CHAPTER 5

MEAT

MEAT IS popular in Thailand. In ancient times any meat was eaten, including rodents and reptiles!

Today, in descending order of popularity, it is pork, beef and lamb or mutton. Pigs are farmed in most parts of Thailand, although pork is not eaten in the Moslem area in the deep south. Wild boar (called jungle pig) is prevalent in the forested hill areas, particularly in the north, as is venison.

Beef is universally popular with both the majority Buddhists and minority Christians and Moslems. It is not eaten by the minority Hindus, to whom the cow is sacred. Beef is less readily available in Thailand than pork, the cattle being smaller and yielding far less meat than their Western counterparts. Buffalo is as popular as cattle, veal is rare, being too expensive. Incidentally, dairy products are rarely used in Thai cooking.

Sheep and goat rearing is virtually non-existent in Thailand except in the Moslem areas. Indeed, most Thais hate the smell and taste of such meat. But mutton and lamb dishes do exist, and I have included one recipe in this chapter specifically for lamb.

Buddhists are not allowed to slaughter meat, Moslems do that task, except for pork which is undertaken by the Chinese. Raw meat is not uncommon, especially in the north Issan district, in the form of a pounded spicy dish called *laab* (*page 50*) lightly resembling our steak tartare.

I should point out that you can substitute any meat for any other in most of these recipes.

I have chosen a diverse selection of dishes in this chapter, and I hope you will try them all, including the frogs' legs with sweet basil on page 98.

LOOK CHEEN PING
Meat Balls on Skewers

Look Cheen Ping literally means 'balls, Chinese, skewered'. Also known as Pad Look Cheen ('fried balls Chinese') or Tod Man Nua ('fried balls, meat'), I hope by now you've got the picture, including the fact that the Chinese had an influence. Meat balls are a very popular street food, either grilled, deep fried or oven baked. They make great snacks or starters, or can be served as part of the main course.

—————————— MAKES: 16 MEAT BALLS ——————————

500g (18 oz) raw ground beef, pork or chicken mixture (*pages 50 and 51*)

1 tablespoon 'magic paste' (*page 42*)
50g (1¾ oz) spring onion leaves, very finely chopped
deep-fry oil

1   Mix the raw mixture with the paste and the spring onion leaves.
2   Divide the mixture into half and half again to make 4 equal size lumps.
3   Take one lump and divide that into 4 and roll into balls. Repeat until you have 16 balls.
4   Heat the deep fry oil to 190°C and put 8 balls into the oil, one at a time (too many too fast lowers the oil temperature). Fry for 6 to 8 minutes. Remove and rest on kitchen paper.
5   Repeat with the other 8 balls.
6   Put 4 balls on to each skewer. Serve hot or cold.

CHEF'S TIP: *These can be oven baked following the recipes on pages 50 and 51, or grilled.*

CORIANDER

NAEM
Chiang Mai Sausage

Several kinds of sausages are found in the north-east of Thailand. Many are enjoyed raw. This is not to our taste, so here is my Westernized version of Naem, using butcher-made sausages. You 'de-case', them and mix the sausage meat with further ingredients, then re-case them and, hey presto! The problem of grinding meat to a paste and making a casing is solved in one! Please note: because you're adding other items, there will be some excess sausage meat, which can be used as a basic for the recipe on page 50.

MAKES: 16 SAUSAGES

16 pork or beef sausages with 80 per cent meat content
100g (4oz) cooked rice
2 tablespoons 'magic paste' (*page 42*)
2.5cm cube of ginger, finely chopped
4 tablespoons chopped spring onion leaves
1 tablespoon fish sauce (*page 36*)
1 teaspoon shrimp paste (*page 36*)
1 teaspoon red curry paste (*page 137*)

1   Without separating the sausages from their 'strings', very carefully empty the sausage meat into a mixing bowl. Since you only need about three-quarters of the meat, remove about one quarter of it and freeze or use for something else.
2   Add the other ingredients into the bowl and mix well.
3   Now comes the tricky bit. You have to pump the mixture back into the sausage skins. The best tool is a food syringe – alternatively, use an icing bag and large nozzle. Take care doing it. Leave a little space between each sausage to allow for twisting the case. And don't overfill them.
4   To cook, preheat the oven to 190°C/375°F/Gas 5. Put the sausages onto a greased oven tray and cook for 45 minutes. Don't prick them unless you want them to burst.
5   Serve as part of the main course, or as a snack or starter.

CHEF'S TIP: *You can purchase sausage skins from butchers who make their own sausages.*

MOO GROB KAEP
Crispy Fried Pork with Crackling

Roast pork is absolutely exquisite when its skin is properly cooked. It is crispy and crunchy and we call it crackling. Also called Moo Grob, Thai people adore this treat too, but without ovens they create it in different ways, the best of which – for the crispiest results – is deep-frying. This has the extra benefit of removing excess fat. Serve it as an accompaniment or garnish, or mixed into other dishes. Pork rind can be obtained from any butcher. It is easiest to buy it by size rather than by weight.

MAKES: 36 PIECES

**Piece of pork rind, totalling about 18cm x 18cm
deep-fry oil**

1   Cut the rind into 36 bite-sized pieces, each about 3cm x 3cm.
2   Heat the deep-fryer to 190°C (chip-frying temperature). One by one put about 18 pieces of rind into the fryer. Fry until pale golden (the time will vary according to the thickness of the rind and its fattiness – so between 8 to 12 minutes).
3   Remove from the fryer. Rest on kitchen paper.
4   Repeat with the other batch.
5   Leave to rest. Keep it warm for about 10 minutes during which time it will crisp up. Serve warm.

LIME LEAVES

SI-KHRONG MOO TOD
Deep-Fried or Barbecued Ribs

Barbecued ribs are, of course, a world class, world-wide phenomenon, as likely to be found in Paris as in Beijing. Pork is the meat, marination is the game, and it is of course, a Chinese speciality. It is equally at home in Thailand, where the marinade is deliciously Thai.

An alternative Thai name for the dish is Grat Dook Moo Tod. Our alternative name is spare ribs. There is nothing spare about this dish. It is good at any time and easy enough to make.

--------------------- MAKES: 8 RIBS ---------------------

8 pork spare ribs (each weighing about 100 – 110g (4oz))

--------------------- THE MARINADE ---------------------

**200ml (7 fl oz) thin coconut milk (*page 35)*
1 tablespoon fish sauce (*page 36*)**

**2 teaspoons palm or brown sugar
2 teaspoons puréed garlic
2 teaspoons red curry paste (*page 137*)**

--------------------- GARNISH ---------------------

**fresh coriander leaves, chopped
snipped chives**

1   Mix the marinade ingredients together in a large, non-metallic bowl.
2   Lightly score the flesh of the ribs. Ensure they are well coated with the marinade. Cover the bowl with film and leave it in the fridge for 24 to 48 hours.
3   To cook, preheat the grill to medium. Line the grill pan with foil. Put the pan rack into place.
4   Shake off any excess marinade (keep it for later) and place the ribs on to the rack. Place the grill pan in the midway position.
5   Grill for 5 minutes. Remove, turn the ribs, and baste them with spare marinade.
6   Grill for 3 more minutes. Baste again (if you have any remaining marinade) and grill for a final 3 to 5 minutes until cooked right through, and slightly singed.
7   Garnish and serve.

TUA LUEANG JEOW
Soya Beans with Pork and Prawns

This combination of meat and shellfish is much adored in Thailand. Here we use lean, coarsely minced pork (though minced beef, veal or chicken would be equally good) and small prawns. This combination is augmented with tinned soya beans, and delicious Thai flavourings.

SERVES: 4

350g (12oz) coarsely minced lean pork

250g (9oz) small shelled cooked prawns

3 tablespoons sunflower or soya oil

400ml (14 fl oz) tinned coconut milk

2 teaspoons fish sauce (*page 36*)

1 tablespoon lemon grass, crosscut (*page 30*)

200g (7oz) tinned soya beans (black or yellow)

1 or more green chillies, chopped

2 tablespoons basil leaves, chopped

GARNISH

fresh coriander leaves
some toasted peanuts

1   Heat the oil in your wok. Add the pork and stir-fry for 2 or 3 minutes.
2   Add the coconut milk, fish sauce and lemon grass and bring to the simmer.
3   Simmer for 20 minutes, stirring from time to time. Add a little water at any time if it seems too dry.
4   Drain the soya beans and add them and the remaining ingredients to the wok and simmer for 10 to 15 more minutes.
5   Garnish and serve.

FACING PAGE   Top to bottom: Rice Salad (page 156), Red Chilli Sauce (page 169), Pickled Mustard, left (page 174) and Malay-style Beef Curry (page 145).

FACING NEXT PAGE   Thailand's favourite Green Curry with Chicken (page 140) with Rice Noodles Salad with King Prawn, Mango and Orange (page 162) and Black and White Rice (page 152). In the foreground is Thailand's national flower, the orchid, and two Chilli Sauces (pages 168-170).

PANAENG NUA
Chilli Beef

If I've been a little restrained on chillies throughout this book, then this recipe will make up for it. It is hot so be warned.

———— SERVES: 4 ————

700g (1½lb) lean stewing steak, cut into bite-sized chunks

4 tablespoons sunflower or soy oil

6 white or green cardamoms

5cm piece cassia bark

1 teaspoon 'magic paste' (*page 42*)

1 tablespoon shrimp paste (*page 36*)

250g (9oz) onion, finely chopped

7 to 21 green Thai chillies (cayenne)

300ml (½ pint) thin coconut milk

2 stalks lemon grass, crosscut (*page 30*)

150g (5½oz) toasted peanuts, chopped

4 tablespoons freshly chopped basil leaves

2 tablespoons finely chopped coriander leaves

4 tablespoons chopped spring onion leaves

1 teaspoon palm or brown)sugar (optional)

———— GARNISH ————

red chillies, shredded
snipped chives
some coconut cream (*see page 35*)

1   Heat the oil in a 2.75 litre casserole dish. Stir-fry the 'magic paste' and the shrimp paste for about 1 minute. Add the onions and chilli and stir-fry for about 3 minutes.

2   Add the meat and seal it by stir-frying for 5 to 8 minutes.

3   Stir in the coconut milk and lemon grass and put the casserole (with its lid on) into the oven pre-heated to 190°C/375°F/Gas 5.

4   Remove after 20 minutes. Stir and add a little water if it is too dry. Return to the oven.

5   Remove again after a further 20 minutes, this time stirring in the remaining ingredients.

6   After a further 20 minutes, it has had an hour in the oven and it should be really tender (if not, return to the oven until it is).

7   Test for seasoning, adding more fish sauce if it needs it.

8   Garnish and serve.

NUA TOD KRAPAO GROB
Crispy Fried Beef and Holy Basil

As I described on page 82, Dominique and I were enjoying a truly magnificent open-air dinner buffet at Bangkok's river bank Shangri-La Hotel. This delightful light stir-fry was one of the dishes we chose. On the table next to us were 10 young enthusiastic Japanese salesmen. They were evidently entertaining their two Thai guests, and trying hugely to impress them. The Singha beers flowed as fast as the adjacent river, and the food was equally abundant. It wasn't long before a clutch of cameras appeared, and in a pass-the-parcel scene, amid much giggling, everyone snapped everyone. The call went up for a group shot. Being the nearest 'volunteer', I was conscripted as cameraman. 'Say cheese', I said. To a man, the 10 Japanese replied 'Cheeser'!

SERVES: 4

600g (1¼lb) lean fillet steak, weighed after stage 1

200g (7oz) holy basil leaves

4 tablespoons sunflower or soya oil

4 cloves garlic, sliced

2.5cm cube of ginger or galangal, shredded

8 tablespoons crispy fried onion (*page 48*)

2 teaspoons fish sauce (*page 36*)

1 tablespoon cross-cut lemon grass (*page 30*)

1 teaspoon palm or brown sugar (optional)

---

1   Deep fry the basil leaves, following the recipe on page 133.

2   Divest the steak of any unwanted matter. Cut it into thin strips about 4cm x 2cm x 4mm each.

3   Heat the oil in your wok. Add the garlic and ginger and stir-fry for 30 seconds.

4   Add the meat strips and briskly stir-fry for about 3 minutes, turning from time to time. You are trying to achieve a colour just browner than pink, for maximum tenderness.

5   Add all the remaining ingredients except the basil and stir-fry for two minutes.

6.   Add the deep-fried basil leaves, toss together then place them into a serving bowl.

7.   Garnish and serve.

NOTE: *To cut meat into thin strips see Chef's Tip page 81.*

NUA-LOOK-GAA PAD BAI-SALANAI
Lamb Stir-fried with Mint

Lamb is scarce in Thailand, and it is true to say that most Thais will never eat it. Flocks of sheep are found where there are Thai Moslems, generally near the Malay border.

I encountered a recipe similar to this at the Gypsy World seaside restaurant. It nestles in the coconut palms of Phuket's Siray (Ko-Sire) island. Known for its Buddha surveying the scene in recline on its hilltop, and its sea gypsy village and sea food, it was an unlikely place to find lamb. This recipe calls for coconut. When the chef calls for it, assistants simply pluck them from the trees. I think this restaurant is probably the luxury I'll have on my own desert island.

SERVES: 4

700g (1½lb) lean leg of lamb, weighed after stage 1

4 tablespoons sunflower or soy oil

5cm cube of ginger or galangal, shredded

50g (1¾oz) tinned sliced bamboo shoot

200ml (7 fl oz) thick coconut milk

6 or 7 spring onions, bulbs and leaves, cross-cut

1 or more green chillies, shredded

4 tablespoons freshly squeezed lime juice

1 teaspoon fish sauce (*page 36*)

1 teaspoon light soy sauce

6 tablespoons chopped fresh mint leaves

GARNISH

some fried cashew nuts
red chilli tassels
fried garlic (*page 45*)

1   Divest the lamb of any unwanted matter. Cut it into thin strips about 4cm x 2cm x 4mm each.

2   Heat the oil in your wok. Briskly stir-fry the lamb strips for about 4 to 5 minutes.

3   Add the ginger and bamboo shoots and enough of their liquid to stop the sizzling.

4   Stir-fry for a further 2 minutes then add the remaining ingredients.

5   When simmering, garnish and serve.

GOHP PAD HORAPA
Frogs' Legs with Sweet Basil

I persuaded a taxi driver to take me to Bangkok's Chatuchak weekend market, with the help of a few hundred more Bhats (the local currency) than he deserved. To be fair, he had kept saying 'far far'. I eventually fell in that this actually meant, 'did I want the fast route' The perpetual traffic jams take their toll on morale, but the extra money pays for the faster toll roads, it seems. But before I reached them the driver sped into a petrol station saying 'waterloo – one minute please'. It took a few bewildered seconds to realize what he meant. Having relieved himself I soon found myself at the market. There in 16 acres of stalls you'll find every conceivable item for sale, including a huge animal section. There I saw tiny puppies, rodents, baby chicks (dyed blue and pink), all sorts of fish, giant black scorpions, snakes, ducks and huge gulping frogs. 'Good to eat,' urged one trader. In the absence of a cooker and a good recipe, I declined. I later did find a good recipe and here it is, for those who enjoy frogs' legs.

SERVES: 4

8 frogs' legs on the bone	chopped
4 tablespoons sunflower or soy oil	3cm cube of ginger or galangal, shredded
3 teaspoons fried garlic (*page 45*)	2 teaspoons fish sauce (*page 36*) 200ml (7 fl oz) chicken stock
8 tablespoons fried onion with prawn (*page 48*)	(*page 43*)
1 or more green chillies,	6 tablespoons chopped holy basil leaves

1   Heat the oil in your wok. Add the garlic, onion, chilli and ginger and stir-fry for about 2 minutes.
2   Add the fish sauce and stock. When simmering, add the frogs' legs.
3   Stir-fry for 10 to 12 minutes at the simmer. The stock will reduce somewhat, but keep the liquid balance by adding a little water now and again.
4   Add the basil. Raise the heat. Stir-fry for a further 5 or 6 minutes. Check that the legs are cooked and serve.

CHEF'S TIP: *Frogs' legs are about the size of chicken drumsticks, their flesh is white and the texture resembles chicken. They are much more appetising than they sound. They are available ready prepared from game butchers.*

CHAPTER 6

POULTRY AND EGGS

CHICKEN IS very popular in Thailand, and the birds are farmed so prolifically that it is more available than other meat. Most of Thailand's population are farmer villagers and most keep chickens (over 80 per cent). Big cities are supplied by chicken-rearing units, and at the markets, cocks, hens and baby chicks are readily available live, although I am not sure that immersing fluffy yellow one-day-old chicks in pink, purple or green food dye is to be applauded, cute though they look on sale in huge trays.

Poultry is generally cooked on the bone, skin on, in Thailand, for the sake of economy. Apart from grilled or baked recipes, I remove the skin and use filleted chicken. What is to be applauded is the wide diversity of recipes to choose from in Thailand. My choice here includes chicken barbecued, stuffed, livers and a stir-fry. Wild birds are popular from the tiniest to the largest and I've represented that with a quail recipe.

As with chickens, many farmers breed duck, and it is rapidly becoming as popular as chicken.

I believe there is more innovation in the cooking of eggs in Thailand than anywhere else. In this chapter I've given an omelette and a scrambled egg recipe. Thais deep-fry eggs by simply breaking them gently into deep-fry oil. Try that sometime – no recipe needed. Or they poach them by breaking them gently into boiling water. Perhaps the most fascinating egg recipe is Son-in-Law's eggs. All is explained on page 54.

GAI YAANG
Barbecued Chicken

All over Thailand you encounter street traders whose trolleys have stoves with burning coals upon which they are barbecuing chicken pieces. The smells are irresistible and there is always a queue of salivating, jabbering Thais, waiting impatiently for their order to cook. This simple concept, requiring a short marinade then a grilling, originated in the north-east Issan area of Thailand. Try it when you're next barbecuing, though this recipe uses the grill.

SERVES: 4

4 chicken thighs and drumsticks (each in one piece)

THE MARINADE

2 tablespoons sweet soy sauce
2 tablespoons fish sauce
(*page 36*)

200ml (7 fl oz) tinned coconut
milk (*page 35*)
2 teaspoons chilli sauce (*page 169*)

2 teaspoons magic paste (*page 42*)

GARNISH

crispy fried onions with prawns (*page 48*)
some basil leaves, shredded

1   It is optional whether you remove the chicken skin or not. Thais don't, but you'll need to cook the chicken for about 3 to 5 minutes longer if the skin stays on to make it really crispy.

2   Slash the chicken pieces with a sharp knife. This gives more surface area for the marinade to reach.

3   Mix the marinade ingredients in a large non-metallic bowl.

4   Work the marinade into the chicken pieces, including the gashes.

5   Leave them to marinate. If you are in a hurry, 30 minutes will do. If you have time, cover the bowl and leave it in the fridge for 24 to 60 hours (*see page 22*).

6   To cook: preheat the grill to medium heat. Line the grill tray with foil shiny side up (it helps to reflect the heat and keeps the tray cleaner). Put the grill pan rack into the pan.

7   Shake any excess marinade off the chicken (keep it for later). Put the

chicken on to the grill rack and put the pan into the midway position under the grill.

8   Grill for 5 minutes. Turn and baste with spare marinade.

9   Grill for 5 more minutes.

10   Check to see if it is fully cooked. It will probably need 2 to 3 minutes or more a side.

11   Garnish and serve with dips and sauces.

THAI TIP: *Barbecuing will take a little longer but will give the best results. Alternatively, the oven can be used (at 190ºC/375ºF/Gas 5) for 15 to 20 minutes, turning once.*

BABY AUBERGINE

OD GAI SORD-SAI
Stuffed Chicken Breast/Wings

Traditionally, this dish uses chicken wings. Each has the two 'arm' bones and a pointed tip. You have to remove the two bones without tearing or breaking the flesh, thus creating a pouch. Keeping the skin on is essential. I have to say de-boning is not easy – it requires patience, practice and a small, sharp knife. The result is worth the effort. If it is all too much for you, the recipe works almost as well using skinned breast, in which it is easy to create a pouch.

––––––––––––––––––– SERVES: 4 –––––––––––––––––––

12 large or 16 small chicken wings
250g (9oz) raw pork stuffing (*pages 50 and 51*)
4 tablespoons fish sauce (*page 36*)
4 tablespoons soy sauce
2 tablespoons chilli sauce (*page 169*)
4 tablespoons tomato ketchup
1 cupful cornflour (about 200g/7oz)
6 tablespoons coconut milk powder

1 De-bone the wings, creating one piece pouches. Do this by carefully scraping the flesh away from the bones. Start at the end opposite the tip and ease the skin and flesh back as you go. Remember to keep the skin on. When the first bone is revealed, cut and break it away at the joint (keep the bones for stock).

2 Put the stuffing into the pouch, but don't overfill it or it will spill out when cooking. Leave enough space at the top to 'close' the pouch by using the skin as a flap.

3 Mix the sauces and the ketchup together in a mixing bowl. Coat the stuffed wings. Leave them to marinate for 1 to 12 hours (*see page 21*).

4 To cook: preheat the deep-fry oil to 190°C (chip-frying temperature).

5 Mix the flour and coconut powder in a bowl and dab one wing in it. Put it into the deep-fryer.

6 Repeat until the fryer is full (using half the wings). Cook for 12 to 15 minutes (depending on size). Test that the chicken is cooked right through. Shake off excess oil and rest on kitchen paper in a warm place.

7 Repeat with the remainder of the wings.

NOTE: *The amount of filling given above will be more than you need (better too much than too little). Use up any surplus filling by rolling into balls and deep-frying at the same time as the wings.*

GAI PAD MAMUANG-HIMAPAN
Sliced Chicken with Cashews

Cashew nuts grow freely in Thailand. This combination of chicken and cashew with its reddish sweet sauce, laced with fresh green herbs, really makes the most of itself. Use raw, unsalted cashews, and chicken breast for a really quick and easy dish.

--- SERVES: 4 ---

500g (18oz) skinned chicken breast

200ml (7fl oz) sunflower or soya oil

200g (7oz) raw shelled cashew nuts

3 teaspoons crispy fried garlic (*page 45*)

6 tablespoons crispy fried onion (*page 48*)

1 red bell pepper, thinly sliced

1 or more red chillies chopped cross-ways

2 tablespoons chilli jam (*page 170*)

4 tablespoons tomato ketchup

2 teaspoons fish sauce (*page 36*)

1 teaspoon palm or brown sugar

6 tablespoons spring onion leaves, cross-cut

2 tablespoons chopped fresh coriander leaves

4 tablespoons chopped fresh basil leaves

--- GARNISH ---

some snipped chives
some lemon grass, cross-cut

1   Chop the chicken into strips about 4cm x 1cm x 5mm.
2   Heat the oil in the wok and fry the cashew nuts for a few minutes, briskly stirring all the time. They turn golden very quickly and burn even more quickly, so watch for that.
3   When they are golden, quickly remove them from the oil with a slotted spoon, and rest on kitchen paper.
4   Remove most of the oil (keep for other use). You now need about 4 tablespoons which you heat in the wok.
5   Add the chicken strips and stir-fry for about 5 minutes.
6   Add all the remaining ingredients (except the cashews and leaves) and stir-fry for 5 minutes. If it wants to stick, at any time from now on, use just enough stock or water to release it.
7   Add the cashews and leaves and stir-fry for 2 or 3 minutes.
8   Garnish and serve.

TAB GAI PAD PRIG
Spicy Chicken Liver

I happen to think chicken liver has a better taste than lamb or pork liver. In fact, so does duck, goose and turkey liver. Since these are tiny, I collect them up in the freezer until I have enough to use for a recipe. Thais happen to adore chicken liver too, as this rapid stir-fry proves so admirably. The alcohol is a trick used by more than one canny Thai chef. My suggestion is that you have more of the same to refresh you while you stir!

--- SERVES: 4 ---

500g (18oz) chicken (or other poultry) liver

4 tablespoons sunflower or soy oil

4 tablespoons crispy fried garlic (*page 45*)

4 tablespoons crispy fried onion (*page 48*)

1 teaspoon fish sauce (*page 36*)

1 or more red chillies, cross-cut

1 teaspoon palm or brown sugar (optional)

4 tablespoons chopped holy (or purple) basil leaves

1 tablespoon chopped coriander leaves

60ml (2 fl oz) port or madeira

--- GARNISH ---

some snipped chives
some lemon grass, cross-cut

1   Cut the liver into strips, which will vary in length because of the actual liver size, but should be about 1cm x 5mm in thickness.
2   Heat the oil. Add the liver and briskly stir-fry for 3 or 4 minutes.
3   Add the remaining items and continue to stir-fry for 2 minutes (until the liver stops oozing red when rested for a minute or so).
4   Garnish and serve.

NOK KRA-TA PAD PRIG
Chilli Quail

Small birds are eaten all over Thailand. Pigeons, sparrows, and who knows what are all avidly consumed. My favourite small bird is quail. Here is a super recipe of my own. Quail, preferably boned if you can obtain them, are best. Specialist quail farms do sell them boned so ask your game butcher. Here, they are marinated then stuffed, roasted then glazed. It sounds more complicated than it is, but the results are well worth the effort.

--- SERVES: 4 ---

4 boned quail
80g (3oz) raw pork stuffing
  (*pages 50 and 51*)
2 tablespoons chopped

cooked prawns
2 tablespoons very finely chopped
  basil leaves
1 teaspoon lemon grass, cross-cut

--- THE MARINADE ---

4 teaspoons sweet soy sauce
1 tablespoon red curry paste
  (*page 137*)
1 tablespoon tomato ketchup

2 teaspoons fish sauce (*page 36*)
150ml (5 fl oz) thick coconut milk
1 teaspoon chilli sauce (*page 170*)
4 tablespoons clear honey

--- GARNISH ---

some lime leaves, shredded (if available)
some red chillies, shredded
some whole coriander leaves

1   Mix the marinade ingredients together in a non-metallic bowl. Work the marinade into the quail, inside and out. Cover the bowl and refrigerate for 24 to 60 hours (*see page 21*).
2   To cook: preheat the oven to 190°C/375°F/Gas 5.
3   Mix the pork, prawns, leaves and lemon grass together.
4   Carefully put one quarter of the pork mix into the quail, but don't overfill it, or it may spill out during cooking. Repeat with the other quails.
5   Place them on an oven tray, basting with any excess marinade. Bake for 10 minutes.
6   Heat the honey and fish sauce in a small pan. Baste it on to the quail. Bake for a final 5 to 8 minutes.
7   Garnish and serve.

PED TOM PHET
Spicy Duck Casserole

Duck is very popular in Thailand. It is eaten on celebration days, and where duck is concerned any day is a celebration day. Duck is widely bred. Most farmers have some for eggs and meat, and there are an increasing number of duck breeding farms popping up, particularly around the major cities. The duck the Thais breed is an Aylesbury hybrid – white, but less plump than its Western counterpart.

Wherever there are Chinese in Thailand you'll find Peking duck for sale. But there are many Thai recipes using duck. This delight works well, casseroled in the oven.

SERVES: 4
---

4 skinless duck breasts, each weighing about 150g to 200g (5 to 7oz)

2 teaspoons 'magic paste' (*page 42*)

1 teaspoon green curry paste (*page 136*)

4 teaspoons crispy fried garlic (*page 45*)

6 tablespoons crispy fried onion (*page 48*)

4 tablespoons sunflower or soya oil

2cm cube of ginger or galangal, chopped

1 teaspoon shrimp paste (*page 36*)

300ml (½ pint) chicken stock or water (*page 43*)

200ml thick tinned coconut milk

3 tassels lemon grass (*page 30*)

3 to 5 whole lime leaves (if available)

50g (1¾oz) Thai pea aubergines (if available)

1 or more red chillis, shredded

3 or 4 Chinese dried mushrooms (*see Chef's Tip*)

2 teaspoons fish sauce (*page 36*)

1 teaspoon palm or brown sugar (optional)

2 tablespoons very finely chopped coriander leaves

GARNISH
---

4 tablespoons finely chopped basil leaves
some red chillies, shredded

---

1 Cut the duck breasts into bite-sized pieces.
2 Heat the oil in a 2.25 to 2.75 litre casserole pot. Stir-fry the pastes for 30 seconds and the duck pieces for about 5 minutes.

3   Add the garlic, onion, ginger, stock, coconut milk, lemon grass and lime leaves. Put the casserole, lid on, into the oven, preheated to 190°C/375°F/Gas 5.

4   Remove after 20 minutes, stir and add the aubergines, chilli and dried mushrooms, and return to the oven.

5   Add the remaining ingredients and, in the unlikely event it needs it, a little water, stirring well.

6   Give it a final 15 to 20 minutes so it has had a total of 50 to 55 minutes in the oven.

7   Garnish and serve in the pot.

CHEF'S TIP: *To reconstitute dried Chinese mushrooms, discard the stems, place them in a large bowl. Pour in enough boiling water to fill the bowl. Leave to soak for 30 minutes, then drain. Cut into pieces.*

AUBERGINE

KAI JEOW
Thai Omelette (various fillings)

The Thai omelette is, as you'd expect, prepared attractively. No simple round shape for the Thais. It is carefully folded into a square which contains a typically fragrant filling. It makes a good light meal on its own, or it can, of course, be part of a main course. The recipe below is for a single omelette. Double or quadruple the quantities for two or four, etc.

--- MAKES: 1 OMELETTE ---

2 large eggs
2 tablespoons sunflower or
  soy oil
1/2 teaspoon 'magic paste'
  (*page 42*)
1/2 teaspoon shrimp paste
  (*page 36*)
80g (3oz) raw stuffing
  (*pages 50 and 51*)

1 teaspoon crispy fried garlic
  (*page 45*)
1 teaspoon chopped red chilli
1 tablespoon chopped basil leaves
2 cherry tomatoes, quartered
1 tablespoon chopped cooked
  prawns
1 tablespoon cooked sweetcorn
1 tablespoon butter

1   Heat the oil in the wok. Add the pastes and stir-fry for 30 seconds. Add the stuffing and stir-fry for 2 or 3 minutes.
2   Add the garlic, chilli, leaves, tomatoes, prawns and sweetcorn and stir in until it is sizzling brightly.
3   Strain off any liquid (reserving it for stock).
4   Beat the eggs.
5   Heat the butter in a large flat frying pan.
6   Pour the beaten egg into the pan, swirling it round to the edges and cook on medium heat until it firms up.
7   Immediately spread the filling around to a square shape in the centre of the omelette.
8   Now fold the sides in to create a square of about 12cm sides.
9   Carefully turn it over, applying a little heat then remove it. Garnish and serve hot.

HED-FAANG-NU GUB KAI-KUAN
Mushroom with Scrambled Egg

A simple, satisfying snack or TV dinner. Here I'm using tinned straw mushrooms, but you can use any type of fresh mushrooms. Being so simple, I've portioned it for two. Halve for one, double for four. Eat it hot and fresh, or try it cold as a sandwich filler for lunch at your work place – but make plenty, you'll have to share it, or you'll be the envy of your colleagues!

———————————— SERVES: 2 ————————————

3 or 4 large eggs
1 tablespoon butter
1 teaspoon yellow curry paste (*page 138*)
1/2 teaspoon lemon grass cut crossways (*page 30*)
1 or more red chilli

1 teaspoon crispy fried garlic (*page 45*)
1 tablespoon thick coconut milk
5 or 6 straw mushrooms, chopped
1 tablespoon chopped spring onion leaves
1 tablespoon chopped basil leaves
salt to taste

white pepper to taste

———————————— GARNISH ————————————

some snipped chives

1   Heat the butter in a small non-stick pan. Add the paste and stir-fry for 20 seconds. Add the lemon grass, chilli and garlic and stir-fry for 20 seconds more.
2   Add the eggs, unbeaten, and gently work them into the stir-fry.
3   As they start to set, after about a minute, add the coconut milk, mushrooms and the leaves.
4   Season to taste and remove from the pan just prior to it setting really firmly.
5   Garnish and serve hot or cold.

CHAPTER 7

FISH AND SHELLFISH

ARLY ARRIVALS in Thailand settled along the waterways. Fish was, and very much still is, Thailand's major staple. It is eaten fresh and is popular sun-dried. From tiny carp to huge mackerel, it is gutted and boned, pressed flat and salted, then clipped into huge drying frames to dry in the sun. It is kept this way for two weeks, by which time it has become translucent and quite hard. Fish is also skewered and smoked. Dried fish and squid is available from Thai shops, and, when reconstituted, can be used in some of these recipes.

Fish is enjoyed at every meal. For breakfast it is served with rice, at other meals it is served in soups, with salads and noodles and in curries. Thai shellfish has an inexhaustible repertoire of recipes. Of course, it is a flavour which is integral to nearly all Thai dishes via Shrimp Paste (*kapee*). Prawns of all sizes (dried and fresh) appear in most Thai dishes – it's so easy to pop them in while you cook.

In this chapter is a mixture of fish recipes from different Thai regions which are all well worth trying. There is a grilled recipe from the north, and a fried recipe from the south. There is a steamed fish recipe, and the unique Hor Mok Pla where minced fish is steamed in a banana leaf cup.

My recipes in this chapter simply tip the iceberg. But they are favourites of mine. Talai Thai is a popular seafood special, Poo Cha is Thailand's adorable 'beloved' crab, and I could not miss the clam recipe – since clams are indigenous to Thailand.

YAANG PLA CHONABOT
Issan-Style Grilled Fish with Vegetables in a Tart Sauce

The river network and lakes in the north-east Issan district of Thailand abound with freshwater fish. There are numerous freshwater fish on sale at the markets, most never seen in the West. This recipe comes from Chonabot, a town not far from the Laos border. It is famous for its Thai silk and cotton, and especially for tie-dyeing.

———————————— SERVES: 4 ————————————

4 freshwater fish (such as carp, perch, salmon or trout), gutted and
filleted with head off, each weighing about 175g to 200g
(6 to 7oz).

———————————— THE PASTE ————————————

1 teaspoon 'magic paste' (*page 42*)	1 teaspoon red curry paste (*page 137*)
1/2 teaspoon shrimp paste (*page 36*)	150ml (5 fl oz) thick coconut milk 1/2 teaspoon salt

6 tablespoons sunflower or soy oil	(if available)
1 teaspoon oyster sauce	6 Thai aubergines, quartered
2 teaspoons chilli jam (*page 170*)	6 baby sweetcorn, halved longways
300ml (½ pint) fish stock or water (*page 44*)	4 oyster mushrooms, quartered
20 to 24 pea aubergines	1 teaspoon or more fish sauce (*page 36*)
	4 tablespoons chopped basil leaves
	1 tablespoon tamarind purée

1   Mix the paste ingredients together.
2   Smear each of the fish both sides with the paste.
3   Preheat the grill to medium hot. Line the grill tray with kitchen foil (to catch the drips and make cleaning easier). Put the grill rack into the tray. Put the fish on to the rack.
4   Place the tray at the midway position and grill for 8 to 10 minutes. The fish should by then be cooking but not burning.
5   Remove the tray, turn the fish and continue grilling for 5 to 8 minutes.
6   During stages 4 and 5, heat the oil in the wok.
7   Add the oyster sauce and chilli jam, and when sizzling, add the fish stock or water.

8   Bring to the simmer.
9   Add the aubergines, sweetcorn and mushrooms.
10   Season with fish sauce and add the leaves and tamarind, and simmer for about 5 minutes (or until the aubergines are cooked).
11   To serve, put the fish onto their respective serving plates. Pour the sauce and vegetables over the fish and serve at once.

GUNG WAN
Sweet Herbal Prawns

This is a really simple dish and it is one of many which you encounter in Bangkok's Seafood Market Restaurant. Here in a vast, jostling neon-lit supermarket you take your basket and wheel it past displays of fresh fish, or seafood on crushed ice, or live in tanks. Make your choice. Take it to the checkout. Pay and tell them how you'd like it cooked. Take a seat and before long your chosen dishes appear cooked and delicious. Use raw unpeeled prawns for the greatest effect here.

SERVES: 2

16 to 20 uncooked king prawns, with head, tail and shell still on	3 teaspoons palm or brown sugar (optional)
3 tablespoons sunflower or soy oil	2 teaspoons chilli jam (*page 170*)
1 teaspoon 'magic paste' (*page 42*)	2 tablespoons tomato chutney
	100ml (3½ fl oz) fish stock or water (*page 44*)
	1 tablespoon fish sauce (nam pla)

1   Wash the prawns.
2   Heat the oil in the wok. Add the prawns and stir-fry for about 6 to 8 minutes, depending on their size, until they are nearly cooked. Add the remaining ingredients and stir-fry briskly until the prawns are fully cooked and coated with the sauce.

PLA TORT
Crispy Fried Fish

A simple dish which is similar in concept to certain Indian fish dishes. This particular recipe hails from Pattani, which is in the far south of Thailand, close to the Malaysian border. Pattani was once a Portuguese base and has a mainly Moslem population. Pla-too is a type of mullet which abounds in the Gulf of Thailand. It is rubbed with salt and turmeric, then deep fried. The sauce which accompanies it must contain cashew because, according to legend, a beautiful Chinese woman hanged herself from a cashew nut tree, having cast a spell on the adjacent mosque, then under construction, which she didn't want finished. The year was 1578. The mosque remains to this day, unfinished and somewhat derelict, but the curse was not entirely successful, as it has been worshipped in since that time.

SERVES: 2

2 red mullet, gutted and filleted, each about 20cm when the head and tail are removed
4 teaspoons ground sea salt
2 teaspoons turmeric
oil for deep-frying

100ml (3½ fl oz) *nam pla prig* (*page 170*)
100g (3½oz) toasted cashew nuts, chopped
4 tablespoons chopped holy basil leaves
lime wedges

1   Wash and dry the fish inside and out, and cut small gashes into flesh.
2   Mix the salt and turmeric together and rub this liberally into the fish.
3   Heat the deep-fry oil to 190°C (chip-frying temperature). Place both fish into the oil and deep-fry for about 10 minutes.
4   During stage 5, mix together the *nam pla prig*, cashews and leaves.
5   Serve the fish with lime wedges and the cashew sauce.

HOI-LAI PHET
Spicy Clams

Clams are a hard hinged double shell (bivalve) part of the mollusc family. They are native to Thailand and China – the first recorded use being in a Chinese census dated AD754, which advises us that the inhabitants of the River Yangtze fished for Venus clams. Clams are available fresh and frozen, in large, medium and small sizes. Medium (also called petite neck) are specified in this recipe, yielding about 50 clams in shell to the kilo. Their meat is plump and creamy in colour.

SERVE: 4

1 kilo (2¼lb) medium size clams in shell
2 tablespoons oil
1 teaspoon 'magic paste' (*page 42*)
1 teaspoon fish sauce (*page 36*)
1 teaspoon chilli sauce (*page 169*)
200ml (7 fl oz) fish stock (*page 44*)
1 stalk lemon grass cross-cut (*page 30*)
1 tablespoon chopped basil leaves

1   Thaw the clams if frozen. Give them a good rinse under cold running water to remove any grit or shell fragments.
2   Steam them for between 5 and 7 minutes. As they start opening, remove them from the steamer. If any fail to open after, say, 10 minutes, discard them .
3   Heat the oil in your wok. Add the magic and chilli pastes and stir-fry for 30 seconds.
4   Add the stock or water and the lemon grass, and when simmering add the clams, and stir-fry for up to 2 minutes.
5   Add the leaves and the fish sauce, simmer for a minute longer then serve hot.

PLA NUENG PRIG MANAU
Spicy Steamed Fish with Lime

A Chinese bamboo steamer is the perfect container for steaming fish. Use any smaller flat white fish such as plaice, lemon and Dover sole, brill, dab, flounder, magrim, skate and witch sole.

_____ SERVES: 2 _____

2 flat white fish (see above), gutted, but not filleted, each weighing about 300g (11oz)
2 teaspoons 'magic paste' (*page 42*)
2 stalks lemon grass, cross-cut
2 stalks lemon grass in tassels
3 lime leaves
2 sticks celery, chopped
2 whole green chillies
2 tablespoons sunflower or soy oil

2.5cm cube of ginger or galangal in thin strips
1 teaspoon yellow curry paste (*page 138*)
1 teaspoon palm or brown sugar (optional)
40ml (1½ fl oz) *nam pla prig* (*page 170*)
100ml (1½ fl oz) fish stock (*page 44*) or water
1 pickled lime, chopped (*page 173*)

_____ GARNISH _____

field mushrooms, in strips
chilli shredded

red bell pepper in strips
spring onion leaves in strips

lime wedges

1   Wash and dry the fish inside and out. Pack its pouch with the paste and the cross-cut lemon grass.
2   Bring 1.5 litres water to a rolling simmer, adding the lemon grass tassels and lime leaves.
3   Put the fish into the steamer basket (one fish per basket) along with the celery and chilli.
4   Put the lidded baskets above the simmering water, for 15 minutes.
5   Meanwhile, heat the oil in the wok. Stir-fry the ginger and curry paste for 30 seconds. Add the sugar, *nam pla prig* and fish stock and simmer for about 10 minutes during which time it should reduce to a thickish sauce. Add the pickled lime.
6   To serve, pour the sauce carefully onto the dinner plates, place the fish on top, garnish with the strips of mushroom, chilli, red pepper and spring onions with a lime wedge.

TALAI THAI
Thai Seafood Special

Seafood is a matter of great importance to the Thais. When you walk around the markets, wherever you are, you'll find a vast array of produce, which if it's not still alive, you know was fished just hours before. It is a rare luxury in the West, unless you live near a fishing port with quay-side markets. We rely on refrigeration, or even freezing, with the consequent deterioration in taste. There is no better way to cook fish and shellfish than over coals, and this recipe works no better than with fresh produce, which benefits from its quick marinade. Of course, the grill or the oven can substitute.

──────────── SERVES: 2 ────────────

2 jumbo prawns, each weighing 100g (3½oz) after
  peeling
6 king prawns, weighing a
  total of about 150g (5½oz)
  after peeling

1 small cleaned squid body
  (about 12cm long) cut into rings
8 mussels in shells
8 scallops out of their shells
4 fresh sardines, whole, each about
  10cm long

24 to 30 whitebait

──────────── THE MARINADE ────────────

2 tablespoons soy oil
2 tablepoons fish sauce
  (*page 36*)
2 teaspoons minced garlic
2 tablespoons soy sauce
2 teaspoons panaeng curry
  paste (*page 138*)

2 teaspoon chilli sauce
  (*page 169*)
1 teaspoon oyster sauce
1 egg
2 tablespoons freshly squeezed
  lime juice
200ml (7 fl oz) thin coconut milk

1   Mix the marinade ingredients together in a large non-metallic bowl.
2   Wash and dry the seafood. Place it all into the marinade. Cover and leave in a cool place for 1 hour.
3   Preheat the barbecue to white hot (or preheat the grill to medium or the oven to 190°C / 375°F / Gas 5).
4   Place the items on the barbecue and cook until ready. These items are gorgeous with fresh crispy baguettes, salad and cold rosé wine on a hot summer's day.

HOR MOK PLA
Ground Fish in Banana Leaf

This dish is immensely popular in Thailand, though it is rarely seen in restaurants outside the country. I particularly like it, or perhaps I should say them. For they are fish cakes. And they are more cake-like than the fish cakes we are used to in the West, or even those on page 67. They are made from a batter which, when steamed, sets and rises a little. Traditionally the batter is poured into moulds made from banana leaves (*see page 52*), but if you don't have banana leaves, dariole moulds will do, though they obviously lack the charm. In order to create a green surround I've used an untraditional method which is to line the mould with spinach leaves.

—————————— SERVES: 4 ——————————

200g (7oz) filleted cod steak
150g (5½oz) cooked peeled prawns, chopped

—————————— THE PASTE ——————————

4 tablespoons chopped spring onions, leaves and bulbs
1 teaspoon 'magic paste' (*page 42*)
2 teaspoons green curry paste (*page 136*)
1 teaspoon shrimp paste (*page 36*)
1 tablespoon lemon grass, finely cross-cut
1 egg
200ml (7 fl oz) thick coconut milk
1 teaspoon rice flour
1 tablespoon fish sauce (*page 36*)
1 or more red chilli, very finely chopped
1 tablespoon chopped basil leaves
8 to 12 spinach leaves

—————————— TOPPING ——————————

6 tablespoons thick coconut milk
2 tablespoons coconut milk powder
1 tablespoon rice flour

—————————— GARNISH ——————————

lime leaves, shredded
snipped chives
red chilli

1   Mix the paste ingredients together in a food processor and grind to a thick pourable paste. Add the cod and prawns and pulse it, using just enough water to maintain the pourable paste.

2   Soften the spinach leaves in the microwave or steamer. Line them into the dariole mould (spinach can be omitted if you use banana leaves).

3   Pour enough mixture into each container to come to 5mm below the top.

4   Mix the topping ingredients together and spoon this to fill each container.

5   Bring 1.5 litres water to a rolling simmer, adding the lemon grass tassels.

6   Put the containers into one or more steamer baskets, which you put lids on above the simmering water. Steam for 15 minutes.

7   Garnish and serve.

CHEF'S TIP: *Containers will vary size-wise, so although I have stated 4 containers, you may need more to use up the mixture. They will freeze after stage 4.*

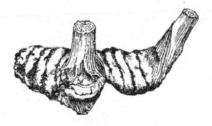

GALANGA

POO CHA
'Beloved Crab'

My wife, Dominique, cannot find anything good to say about crabs. She detests their appearance, the way they move, their smell and their taste. The same goes for all shellfish. Which is unfortunate because I love 'em. So I couldn't agree more with the Thais who go as far as calling this dish their 'beloved crab', or their 'darling' dish.

Crab meat is mixed with ground pork and Thai fragrant ingredients. It is then loaded into the crab shells, coated with beaten egg and fried in the wok in sufficient oil to cover the crabshells.

SERVES: 4

---

2 edible cooked brown crabs, each weighing around 400g (14oz)

THE STUFFING

---

4 tablespoons raw pork stuffing (*page 51*)

1 tablespoon chopped cooked prawns

1 teaspoon shrimp paste (*page 36*)

1 teaspoon 'magic paste' (*page 42*)

1 teaspoon yellow curry paste (*page 138*)

1 or more red chilli, finely chopped

2 tablespoons spring onion leaves

1 teaspoon fish sauce (*page 36*)

500ml (18 fl oz) vegetable oil

2 eggs

GARNISH

---

some snipped chives

---

1   Remove the crab claws and legs. Extract the flesh using pliers and a special pick. Remove and discard the tail, then twist the body out of the shell with a knife. Discard the finger-like grey gills and the stomach behind the eyes. Keep both the white and brown meat. Wash the body shell. Using pliers, crack off the top shell and discard. Wash again. The yield from a 400g (14oz) crab is around 150g to 180g (5 to 6oz).

2   Mix the crab meat with the pork and prawns, pastes, chilli, onion and fish sauce.

3   Press this mixture into the crab shells then chill them in the fridge for at least an hour or overnight (it helps to keep them in the shell at stage 5).

4   Heat the oil in the wok.

5   Beat the eggs. Generously coat one crab. Place it into the wok on its back. Add the second crab.

6   Fry for 10 to 12 minutes. Remove from the wok shaking off the excess oil. Rest on kitchen paper.

7   Garnish and serve hot.

BABY CHILLIES

CHAPTER 8

VEGETABLES

I HAVE TO SAY that, in truth, this chapter is a little 'artificial'. The fact is that few Thais are vegetarian and few Thai dishes turn up on the table as vegetable only. As often as not, they'll have prawn, chicken or meat included. That's not to say that Thai vegetables are not interesting. They are diverse and traditional. By that I mean they are, to this day, largely confined to those vegetables which were indigenous to Thailand centuries ago. This includes aubergines, banana, cabbage, celery, cucumber, gourd, mushrooms and spinach. Interlopers from China, far back in time, include beansprouts, bamboo shoots and water chestnuts and the ubiquitous soya bean, in the form of bean proper or tofu.

Within the last couple of decades two newcomers have arrived in Thailand as cash crops – asparagus and baby corn. This selection of vegetable recipes gives a wide range of tastes and textures and one or more dishes can be served with your main course.

One more observation about vegetables. Dominique and I were on the outboard Thai Airways flight to Bangkok on our research trip for this book. The middle-aged couple behind us were particulary irritating during the early part of the long flight. He had put on his headphones and she kept talking to him. Both were deliberately loud in haughty OTT accents. Jarringly so, in fact. Eventually silence fell when they were given the dinner menu.

Steward Isares asked what choice they'd like. The man said, 'Oh, it isn't five courses?'

'No, Sir, they are your choices.' Rather miffed, he ordered the vegetarian option, she, the meat.

Later Isares appeared with the meals, one vegetarian, one meat.

'Sir,' he said, 'you are a vegetable?'

'Yes,' mouthed Dom and I.

PAD PAK RUAN (OR MANGASWARIT)
Stir-Fry Mixed Vegetables

Choose any vegetables which stir-fry quickly. These include: carrot, mushroom, snowpeas, mangetout, green beans, capsicum, beansprouts, Chinese cabbage, white cabbage, spinach, etc.

You should keep the vegetables as crispy and crunchy as possible, to retain all their goodness.

───────────── SERVES: 4 ─────────────

450g (1lb) mixed vegetables (examples above), weighed after preparing
2 tablespoons sunflower or soya oil
1 clove garlic, chopped
1cm cube of ginger or galangal, chopped
1 teaspoon oyster sauce
1 teaspoon fish sauce (*page 36*)
4 tinned water chestnuts, halved, and their liquid
6 slices tinned bamboo shoot, quartered, and their liquid
2 tablespoons chopped red bell pepper
4 or 5 spring onion bulbs and leaves, chopped
2 tablespoons chopped flat bladed parsley
2 tablespoons chopped fresh basil leaf

1   Heat the oil in the wok. Stir-fry the garlic and ginger for 30 seconds. Add the oyster sauce and when sizzling, add the fish sauce, water chestnuts and bamboo and 4 tablespoons of their liquid (keep more for later).
2   When this is simmering add the mixed vegetables and peppers and stir-fry for 2 minutes.
3   Add the spring onion, parsley and basil and 4 more tablespoons of tinned liquid.
4   Stir-fry for 2 more minutes then serve.

THAI TIP: *Freeze the remaining tinned liquid for stock.*

SATU
Vegetable Stew

I only met this dish once on a visit I made to southern Thailand, years ago. I was told it was a 'village' dish with an Indonesian influence. It was here that I was told about Thai peoples' difficulty in combining letters 's' and 't' (*see satay, page 59*). Satu is a 'corruption' of the word stew. The version I encountered was slowly cooked in a brass two-handled wok. I've translated that to a casserole and the oven for perfect results.

SERVES: 4

150g (5½oz) large potatoes, peeled
150g (5½oz) red sweet potatoes (American yams), peeled
100g (3½oz) carrot, peeled
1 medium size onion
4 celery sticks
200g (7oz) fresh sweet corn (when in season)
600ml (1 pint) boiling water
3 or 4 stalks lemon grass cut into tassels (*page 30*)

3 or 4 whole lime leaves
4 tablespoons sunflower or soy oil
1 teaspoon 'magic paste' (*page 42*)
4 tinned tomatoes, chopped
1 tablespoon tomato ketchup
1 teaspoon dark soy sauce
1 teaspoon palm or brown sugar (optional)
1 teaspoon fish sauce (*page 36*)
4 tablespoons chopped spring onions, leaves only
2 tablespoons chopped basil

1   Chop the potatoes and carrot into large pieces.
2   Halve the onion.
3   Cut the celery sticks into longish lengths.
4   Cut the sweetcorn off the cob.
5   Preheat the oven to 190°C/375°F/Gas 5. Boil the water and put it into a 2.25 litre casserole pot with the lemon grass and lime leaves. Add the mixed vegetables and put the pot, lid on, into the oven.
6   After 20 minutes, heat the oil in the wok. Stir-fry the paste for 30 seconds, add the tomatoes, the ketchup, soy, sugar and fish sauce and when sizzling, transfer it to the casserole, mixing it in well.
7   After a further 15 minutes the potatoes should be cooked (if not carry on casseroling until they are). Add the spring onions and the basil.
8   Let it stand for about 5 minutes, lid on, out of the oven.
9   Serve with rice or noodles.

NAM PRIG ONG
Northern Chilli Vegetables

Also called Pak Nam Prig, this dish is a northern Thai speciality. I encountered it near the Burmese border, where it is a simple staple. The vegetables are raw – crudités – and are dipped into a searingly hot chilli sauce in which, often as not, there will be minced pork. Here I've substituted minced mooli (white radish) to make it a vegetable dish (albeit with shrimp paste and fish sauce).

SERVES: 4

THE VEGETABLES

Your choice of crudités for example: cauliflower and/or broccoli florets, spring onions, celery sticks, carrots, peppers, chillies, cucumber, baby sweetcorn, etc. Judge the amount you want to serve by eye rather than weight.

THE SAUCE

250g (9oz) white radish (mooli)

3 tablespoons sunflower or soy oil

2 cloves garlic, very finely chopped

1 teaspoon shrimp paste (*page 36*)

1 teaspoon chilli sauce (*page 169*)

1 teaspoon fish sauce (*page 36*)

1 tablespoon tomato chutney

4 tinned tomatoes, chopped

1 or more tablespoons chopped tiny red Thai chillies (or Indian cayennes)

2 tablespoons chopped fresh coriander leaves

4 tablespoons chopped fresh basil

---

1   Wash and prepare the vegetables. They are best in sticks or strips or chunky for dipping. Arrange them as individual portions on 4 side plates.
2   Run the white radish through a hand or electric mincer.
3   Heat the oil in the wok and stir-fry the paste for 30 seconds.
4   Add the fish sauce, tomato chutney, tomatoes and chilli and stir-fry for 3 or 4 minutes.
5   Add the minced radish, the coriander and the basil. Mix in well. Remove the wok from the heat and serve the sauce hot or cold, alongside the crudités.

GALUMBI HAR TAO-HOU
Tofu Wrapped in Cabbage Leaves

Although this and the next recipe are the only encounters with tofu, or *tao-hou*, in this book (*see page 39*), it is not to imply that tofu is a minor ingredient in Thai cuisine. It appears here, there and everywhere as do other ingredients such as minced pork and prawns, and there is nothing to prevent you adding tofu to virtually any savoury dish in this book.

Here it features as a major ingredient, in a typically attractive Thai presentation, so pretty it's well worth the effort to make. Soft bean curd (tofu), available from Chinese or Thai stores, is moulded with flavourings to a sausage shapes, softened cabbage leaves are tightly formed round the sauages. Thai garlic chive leaves (or long halved spring onion leaves) are then rolled decoratively round the sausage, which is then steamed.

MAKES: 8

12 large Chinese leaves	2 teaspoons very finely chopped
16 long garlic chives	garlic
300g (10½oz) fresh soft white	1 tablespoon chopped basil
unsalted bean curd (tofu)	1 teaspoon chopped red chilli
100g (3½oz) thick cottage	1 tablespoon chopped coriander
cheese	leaves
1 egg	1/2 teaspoon salt
	lime wedges

1 Steam the leaves and chives until they are soft and translucent but do not overcook them.
2 Discard the water from the tofu.
3 Mash it with the cottage cheese, egg, garlic, basil, chilli and coriander and salt.
4 Divide it into 8 and mould into sausages.
5 Place one sausage onto a cabbage leaf, fold the leaf over the ends and form it into the tofu sausage. Note there are spare leaves in case of tears, etc.
6 Now wrap the long chives around the sausage.
7 Put into the steamer and cook for about 5 minutes.
8 Serve hot or cold with lime wedges.

HED GUB TAU-HOU KHAENG
Spicy Mushroom with Tofu

A traditional combination with pleasing results of colour contrasts (black, grey and white) and chewy textures. Use several types of fresh mushroom for greatest effect. Examples include field, button, beefsteak, straw and oyster mushrooms. Several varieties are often available in mixed packs at supermarkets. The tofu is available in blocks.

_____ SERVES: 4 _____

200g to 250g (7 to 9oz) mixed fresh mushrooms (*see above*)
200g (7oz) firm tofu
2 tablespoons sesame oil
2 teaspoons white sesame seeds

1 teaspoon 'magic paste' (*page 42*)
4 to 6 spring onion bulbs and leaves, cross-cut
150ml (¼ pint) vegetable stock or water
1 teaspoon fish sauce (*page 36*)

1   Clean the mushrooms, peeling only if necessary.
2   Cut them into larger rather than small pieces.
3   Cut the tofu into cubes about 1.5cm square.
4   Heat the oil in the wok. Stir-fry the seeds and paste for 30 seconds. Add the tofu and when sizzling, add the onion, stock and fish sauce.
5   When simmering, add the mushrooms.
6   Stir-fry for a couple of minutes (until everything is hot) then serve.

DOON NAW-MAI-FARANG
Steamed Asparagus

It has to be fresh asparagus, of course. So when the season comes, do what the Thais do and enjoy it at any and every meal. For breakfast with scrambled duck eggs it's astounding. Use the tastier green variety in preference to the white. For brunch lunch or munch, just try it!

SERVES: 4

approx 900g (2lb) bunch of asparagus
3 tablespoons sunflower or soy oil
1 clove garlic, chopped
1 teaspoon fish sauce (*page 36*)
1 teaspoon light soy sauce

1 teaspoon palm or brown sugar (optional)
1/2 teaspoon ground white pepper
150ml (5 fl oz) vegetable stock or water
some knobs of butter
holy basil leaves

1   Cut the stalks away from the asparagus where it becomes tough and discard it.
2   Steam the asparagus for about 15 minutes or microwave it for about 3 minutes. (Don't boil it – it becomes mushy and loses flavour.)
3   Heat the oil in the wok. Stir-fry the garlic for 30 seconds. Add the fish and soy sauces and the sugar and pepper.
4   When sizzling, add the stock or water and stir-fry for about 3 minutes to enable it to reduce to a thicker consistency.
5   To serve, place the asparagus into a serving dish and pour the sauce over it. This minimizes the risk of breaking the fragile tips. Garnish with butter and fresh holy basil leaves.

KAO-POT PAK-BOONG PAD
Stir-Fried Sweetcorn and Spinach

Sweetcorn is hugely popular in Thailand. And it's not just baby corns. Gorgeous, golden, plump, full size corn-cobs grow prolifically for much of the year and their flavour is just out of this world.

This recipe combines these golden nuggets with the velvety green of Thai spinach (*pak boong*) also called, rather unglamorously, swamp cabbage because it grows in swampy sites! It has a rather more attractive name – water morning glory. It has narrow triangular leaves, and hollow stems, both of which are used in this recipe, and is available from time to time fresh in Thai or Chinese shops where it is known as *kaeng kung*. Failing that use ordinary young spinach with soft usable stalks.

SERVES: 4

300g (10½oz) swamp cabbage (*pak-boong*) or spinach coarsely chopped
200g (7oz) fresh sweetcorn kernels
4 tablespoons sunflower or soy oil

4 cloves garlic, chopped
150ml water
1 teaspoon fish sauce (*page 36*)
1 teaspoon palm or brown sugar (optional)
1 teaspoon chopped red chilli (Thai or cayenne)

1   Steam, boil or microwave the sweetcorn to readiness.
2   Heat the oil in the wok, stir-fry the garlic for 30 seconds.
3   Add the water, fish sauce, sugar, chilli and the swamp cabbage and briskly stir-fry for about 3 minutes.
4   Add the sweetcorn. Stir-fry until it is hot then serve.

MAKHUA BREEO-WAN
Sweet and Sour Aubergine

There are a number of Thai aubergine varieties, one of which is the shiny club-shaped purple-black variety so popular in India. Other Thai types vary from the small green 'pea aubergines' (*makhua puong*) to the larger cream or yellow varieties. Called just *makhua*, one can see why they are called egg plants, since they are that shape. No Thai cookbook would be complete without a recipe for aubergine.

Available from Thai shops, they are actually somewhat bitter especially the pea version.

To overcome this you should soak the aubergines in brine. This sweet and sour recipe suits aubergines well.

SERVES: 4

350g (12oz) aubergines, weighed after stage 3	100ml (3½ fl oz) sweet white wine
3 tablespoons sunflower or soy oil	2 tablespoons rice vinegar
2 cloves garlic chopped	2 tablespoons fresh lime juice
4 tablespoons palm or brown sugar	2 tablespoons chopped spring onion leaves
60ml (2 fl oz) water	1 tablespoon chopped holy basil leaves
	salt to taste

1   Put the water and salt together in a large mixing bowl.
2   Add the aubergines (pea aubergines whole and other types peeled and halved with seeds scooped out).
3   Soak them for up to 3 hours then drain them.
4   To cook, steam the aubergines for 12 to 15 minutes (or until tender – it depends on their size).
5   Heat the oil in the wok. Add the garlic and stir-fry for about 30 seconds. Add the sugar and water, white wine and vinegar and stir briskly until the sugar dissolves.
6   At a rolling simmer stir until this becomes more syrupy.
7   Add the aubergine and the remaining ingredients.
8   Stir for a little longer until it thickens, then serve.

NAM PLA WAN PAK-CHEE
Sweet and Sour Coriander

If you adore that musky taste which is coriander as much as the Thais do, then this sweet and sour dish is for you. Coriander alone is not enough to make this a side dish. The addition of Chinese leaves (Galumbi) and optional dry prawns brings out the very best from the coriander.

SERVES: 4

100g (3½oz) dried prawns (optional)
300g (10½oz) Chinese leaves
100g (3½oz) coriander leaves, stems and roots
4 tablespoons sunflower or soy oil
2 teaspoons 'magic paste' (*page 42*)

1 teaspoon shrimp paste (*page 36*)
1 tablespoon tamarind purée (*page 47*)
1 teaspoon fish sauce (*page 36*)
60ml (2 fl oz) sweet white wine or sherry
1 tablespoon palm sugar

GARNISH

2 teaspoons crispy garlic (*page 45*)
4 tablespoons crispy onion (*page 48*)
some holy basil leaves

1   Soak the prawns in ample water for a couple of hours or more.
2   Chop the Chinese leaves into coarse shreds, and the coriander leaves and root rather finer.
3   Heat the oil in the wok. Stir-fry the pastes for 30 seconds. Add the tamarind, fish sauce, wine and sugar.
4   When it is simmering, add the leaves and stir-fry until they are glistening and hot.
5   Drain the prawns, and add them, stir-fry for about 5 minutes.
6   Garnish and serve.

BAI HORAPA TORD GROB
Crisp-Fried Basil Leaves

This is more of a garnish than a fully fledged dish. It is simple, especially when you have the deep-fryer operating. Simply deep-fry fresh basil leaves. In a whoosh, they go really crispy. You can serve these leaves with any other dish and they are superb.

SERVES: 4 AS AN ACCOMPANIMENT

60 or 70 whole Horapa basil leaves, removed from their stalks

1   Heat the deep-fry oil to 190°C (chip-frying temperature).
2   Add enough leaves to cover the surface area of the pan and no more. Press them under the oil with a slotted spoon then release them. They will whoosh up and cook virtually at once.
3   Remove them with the slotted spoon, shaking off excess oil, and rest on kitchen paper.
4   Repeat with the remaining basil.

THAI BASIL

CHAPTER 9

CURRIES

I BELIEVE SOME confusion exsits in the West about Thai curries. Newcomers to the Thai restaurant expect to find a creamy rich Indian-style curry delivered to the table. They are nonplussed with the somewhat watery, but very colourful, fragrant dish which appears.

Thai curries are very spicy being laced with intensely hot chilli. The integral ingredients are ground into a curry paste (*krung*) which can be bought as a factory bottled product. This is fine if you are in a hurry, but they are all, in fact, generally very chilli hot. Fresh ingredients are better. Here I have given recipes for six pastes which are to be used fresh. Four are 'colour-coded' – red, green, yellow and orange and these are four of the most popular Thai curries. Two pastes are for southern Thai curries which are influenced by Malay Indians, and are nearest to Indian curries (especially the Mussaman curry). Both of these are known as *karee* or *guri* (curry) whereas the Thai word for curry is *khaeng* – literally meaning spicy liquid.

The six recipes which follow are one of each curry, each with a different main ingredient. However, any of the curries can be cooked with any main ingredient, so feel free to mix and match.

A final word about Thai curries (apart from the fact that they are absolutely delicious, and that you should serve at least one with every main course), is that you'll find hawkers and restaurants in Thailand called *Khao Khaeng*. It literally means 'curry over rice', and since its a meal in itself, I suggest you try one now for yourself.

KRUNG KHAENG
Curry Pastes

Thai Curry pastes

Each of the six recipes below will give you enough curry paste to make one curry (which serves four). It is much better to make your paste up freshly each time. It not only gives the dish a brighter colour, but it tastes brighter, too.

The method for making the paste is the same for five of the six:

KRUNG KHAENG KEO-WAN
Green Curry Paste

─────── MAKES: ENOUGH PASTE FOR ONE GREEN CURRY ───────

2 tablespoons sunflower oil
2 tablespoons chopped green bell pepper
1 to 7 green cayenne chillies
3cm ginger or galangal, chopped
60g (4oz) spring onion leaves
2 cloves garlic, halved
1 teaspoon fish sauce (*page 36*)

½ teaspoon ground coriander seed
½ teaspoon ground cummin
1 tablespoon chopped fresh coriander leaf shredded
1 teaspoon very finely chopped lemon grass
½ teaspoon shrimp paste (*page 36*)

1   Mulch everything down in the food processor, using just enough water to achieve a thick paste.

KRUNG KHAENG PED DAENG
Red Curry Paste

--- MAKES: ENOUGH PASTE FOR ONE RED CURRY ---

2 tablespoons sunflower oil

2 tablespoons chopped red bell pepper

1 to 7 red cayenne chillies

3cm ginger or galangal, chopped

60g (4oz) carrot, chopped

2 teaspoons paprika

1/2 teaspoon ground coriander

1/2 teaspoon ground cummin

2 tablespoons holy purple basil (if available)

1 lime leaf shredded (if available)

1 teaspoon very finely chopped lemon grass

1/2 teaspoon shrimp paste (*page 36*)

1 teaspoon fish sauce (*page 36*)

1   Mulch everything down in the food processor, using just enough water to achieve a thick paste.

KRUNG KHAENG SOM
Orange Curry Paste

--- MAKES: ENOUGH PASTE FOR ONE ORANGE CURRY ---

2 tablespoons sunflower or soy oil

3 tablespoons chopped orange bell pepper

1 to 7 orange Thai chillies

3cm ginger or galangal, chopped

60g (4oz) carrot, chopped

1cm fresh turmeric root (if available), chopped

or 1/3 teaspoon ground turmeric

1/2 teaspoon ground coriander

1/2 teaspoon ground cummin

1 tablespoon chopped fresh coriander leaves

1 teaspoon very finely chopped lemon grass

1 teaspoon shrimp paste (*page 36*)

1 teaspoon fish sauce (*page 36*)

1   Mulch everything down in the food processor, using just enough water to achieve a thick paste.

KRUNG KHAENG LEUNG
Yellow Curry Paste

MAKES: ENOUGH FOR ONE YELLOW CURRY

2 tablespoons sunflower oil
3 tablespoons chopped yellow bell pepper
1 or 2 yellow scotch bonnet or Habanero chillies
3cm ginger or galangal, chopped
1cm fresh turmeric root (if available)

or ½ teaspoon ground turmeric
½ teaspoon ground coriander
½ teaspoon ground cummin
1 tablespoon chopped fresh basil leaf
1 teaspoon very finely chopped lemon grass
1 teaspoon shrimp paste (*page 36*)
1 teaspoon fish sauce (*page 36*)

1   Mulch everything down in the food processor, using just enough water to achieve a thick paste.

KRUNG KHAENG PANAENG
Malay-style Curry Paste

MAKES: ENOUGH FOR ONE PANAENG CURRY

2 tablespoons sunflower or soy oil
5 to 7 red cayenne chillies
2 tablespoons chopped red bell pepper
12 cloves garlic, halved
2 teaspoons 'magic paste' (*page 42*)
4cm ginger or galangal, chopped

1 teaspoon ground coriander
½ teaspoon ground cummin
1 teaspoon shrimp paste (*page 36*)
1 teaspoon fish sauce (*page 36*)
1 teaspoon lemon grass, very finely cross-cut (*page 30*)
4 tablespoons chopped spring onion leaves
1 teaspoon green peppercorns (fresh or in brine)

1   Mulch everything down in the food processor, using just enough water to achieve a thick paste.

KRUNG KHAENG GARI MUSSAMAN
Moslem-style Curry Paste

──────── MAKES: ENOUGH FOR ONE MUSSAMAN CURRY ────────

──────────── THE SPICES ────────────

4 cloves	1 teaspoon cummin seeds
2 teaspoons coriander seeds	4 to 6 white or green cardamoms

5cm piece cassia bark

8 to 12 dried red chillies	6 to 8 cloves garlic
2 or 3 dry lime leaves (if available)	3cm cube ginger or galangal
	4 tablespoons chopped onion
2 tablespoons sunflower or soy oil	2 tablespoons lemon grass, very finely cross-cut (*page 30*)
1 teaspoon shrimp paste	1 teaspoon fish sauce (*page 36*)

1   Heat a dry wok on the stove. Put the spices in and dry roast for about a minute, stirring continuously, ensuring nothing burns. Note the aroma!
2   Transfer to a cold bowl and let it cool down.
3   Grind it as finely as you can in an electric coffee grinder, spice mill or mortar and pestle.
4   Put the remaining ingredients into the blender, and using just enough water, mulch them down to a purée.
5   Pulse in the ground spices.
6   Serve with rice.

KHAENG KEO-WAN GAI
Green Curry with Chicken

Green curry is probably Thailand's most popular dish, inside and outside the country. Cooked correctly it is a delicate blend of fragrance and flavour, of subtle colour (it should not be lurid green) laced together with creamy coconut milk. Traditionally, pea aubergines are used in this curry. If these are unavailable, omit them or use other aubergines or even green peas. Here is all of that magic, using chicken.

SERVES: 4

700g (1½lb) skinned chicken breast
20 to 30 pea aubergines
3 tablespoons sunflower or soy oil
1 batch green curry paste (*page 136*)
400ml (14 fl oz) tinned

coconut milk
1 stalk lemon grass, cross-cut
2 or 3 lime leaves, shredded
1 teaspoon fish sauce (*page 36*)
2 tablespoons chopped basil leaves
some fresh chopped coriander leaves

GARNISH

whole and shredded lime leaves

1 Soak then cook the aubergines if you are using them, following steps 1 to 3 of the recipe on page 131.
2 Heat the oil in the wok. Add the green curry paste and stir-fry for about 1 minute.
3 Add the coconut milk, the lemon grass, and lime leaf and simmer for about 5 minutes stirring occasionally to allow the coconut to thicken. It may look as though it is curdling – but it cannot do this so don't worry.
4 Add the chicken and cook for 10 minutes, stirring from time to time.
5 In the unlikely event it thickens up too much, add water as required.
6 Add the cooked aubergines, fish sauce and the leaves. Continue to cook for about 5 more minutes. Test that the chicken is fully cooked by cutting one piece in half which should be white right through.
7 Then garnish and serve.

KHAENG PED-DAENG PLA
Red Curry with Fish

As with the preceding green curry, red curry should be a delicate blend of red ingredients, which when mixed with coconut will give you a subtle red colour (not a lurid one). In this example I am using fish.

—————— SERVES: 4 ——————

700g (1½lb) firm white fillet-ed fish steaks (eg: cod) cut into bite-sized pieces
3 tablespoons sunflower or soya oil

1 batch red curry paste (*page 137*)
400ml (14 fl oz) tinned coconut milk
1 teaspoon fish sauce (*page 36*)

3 tablespoons chopped basil leaves (*manglak* if available)

—————— GARNISH ——————

some strips of red pepper and lime leaves
a few small pink onion strips

1   Heat the oil in a wok. Add the red curry paste and stir-fry for about 1 minute.
2   Add the coconut milk, the lemon grass and lime leaves and simmer for about 5 minutes, stirring occasionally to allow the coconut to thicken. It may look as though it is curdling, but it cannot do this, so don't worry.
3   Add the fish and cook for about 7 to 8 minutes, stirring frequently. If it needs a little water, add it sparingly to keep things mobile.
4   Add the fish sauce and the leaves and continue to cook for about 3 more minutes, or until the fish is fully cooked.
5   Garnish and serve.

KHAENG SOM SUPPAROT GUNG
Orange Curry with Prawns and Pineapple

Yet another colour variant, this one found less often than the previous two. Using orange ingredients and garnished with orange wedges, it produces a most attractive curry. Here, I'm using prawns.

SERVES: 4

600g (1¼lb) peeled cooked prawns, any size

100g (3½oz) fresh pineapple, in bite-sized pieces

3 tablespoons sunflower or soy oil

1 batch orange curry paste (*page 137*)

1 stalk lemon grass cross-cut (*page 30*)

1 teaspoon green peppers in brine

2 or 3 lime leaves, shredded

1 teaspoon fish sauce (*page 36*)

2 tablespoons chopped holy basil leaves

GARNISH

**some orange wedges, pith removed
a green chilli tassel
some snipped chives**

1   Heat the oil in the wok. Stir-fry the orange curry paste for about 1 minute

2   Add the coconut milk, the lemon grass, peppercorns and lime leaves and simmer for about 5 minutes stirring occasionally to allow the coconut to thicken. It may look as though it is curdling, but it cannot do this, so don't worry.

3   Add the remaining ingredients. Stir-fry until they are hot right through.

4   Garnish and serve.

KHAENG LEUNG PA-MOO YAANG
Yellow Curry with Grilled Wild Boar

If you are a gemstone enthusiast, Chanthaburi, the 'City of the Moon', close to Cambodia, is the place to go for rubies and sapphires. You'll also find Vietnamese and Cambodian people, Christianity, smuggling, crabs and noodles. Wildlife also abounds, and there are several national parks, and *pa-moo* (jungle pig or wild boar as we know it), is quite prolific. Here is a yellow curry recipe, using wild boar which is just stupendous, and available from game butchers. Pork can be substituted.

SERVES: 4

750g (1lb 10oz) lean leg of wild boar, weighed after stage 1
2 tablespoons sunflower or soy oil
1 batch yellow curry paste (*page 138*)
250ml (9 fl oz) tinned coconut milk
2 lemon grass stalks, finely cross-cut (*page 30*)
3 or 4 lime leaves, shredded
250ml (9 fl oz) chicken stock (*page 43*)
2 tablespoons sesame oil
1 teaspoon fish sauce (*page 36*)
2 tablespoons chopped basil leaves
1 tablespoon chopped coriander

GARNISH

chopped red chilli
snipped chives

1 Divest the meat of all unwanted matter, then cut it into 4cm by 2cm by 4mm strips.
2 Heat the oil in the wok. Stir-fry the yellow curry paste for about a minute.
3 Add the coconut milk, the lemon grass and the lime leaves and simmer for about 5 minutes, stirring occasionally, to allow the coconut to thicken. It may look as though it is curdling, but it cannot do this, so don't worry.
4 During stage 3 heat the sesame oil in a clean frying pan. Stir-fry the boar strips for about 5 minutes, turning frequently.
5 Add the meat to the wok and continue to stir-fry for about 5 more minutes. During this time add the chicken stock bit by bit.
6 Add the fish sauce and the leaves and stir-fry for a final minute or two. Check that the boar is cooked and tender (it certainly should be by now).
7 Garnish and serve.

KHAENG MUSSAMAN HED GUNG
Moslem-Style Curry with Oyster Mushroom and Prawns

The further south you go in Thailand, the closer you get to the Malaysian border, and the more Thai Moslems you'll find. At the town of Satun, for example, is a gold-domed mosque, near which are a number of *roti khaeng* (Indian flat bread with curry) stalls. One curry you'll be sure to get there is called Mussaman. This curry is the nearest in style to Indian you'll get in Thailand. Here is the typical Mussaman taste with oyster mushrooms and prawns.

SERVES: 4

24 cooked king prawns, peeled but with tail on, each weighing about 22g to 25g (1oz)
4 tablespoons dried prawns
200ml (7 fl oz) fish stock
4 to 6 oyster mushrooms
3 tablespoons sunflower or soy oil

1 batch Mussaman curry paste (*page 139*)
4 tablespoons coconut milk powder
1 stalk lemon grass cut into a tassel (*page 30*)
2 or 3 lime leaves
salt to taste

SPICES

2 star aniseed
2 or 3 white (or green) cardamoms

5cm piece cassia bark
2 or 3 bay leaves

GARNISH

some red chilli in strips or whole
some chopped fresh coriander leaves

1   De-vein and wash the king prawns.
2   Put the dried prawns into the stock and leave them to soak for an hour.
3   Quarter the mushrooms.
4   Heat the oil. Stir-fry the spices for 30 seconds. Add the Mussaman curry paste and continue to stir-fry for a further minute.
5   Add the soaked prawns, the stock, coconut milk powder, lemon grass and lime leaves and bring to the simmer, stirring for a couple of minutes.
6   Add the king prawns and the mushrooms and simmer for 3 more minutes. Salt to taste.
7   Garnish and serve.

KHAENG PANAENG NUA
Malay-style Beef Curry

Traditionally the dish should turn out dryish, its gravy thickened with peanut, its colour deep reddy brown.

SERVES: 4

700g (1½lb) lean stewing steak or leg of lamb, weighed after stage 1
80g (3oz) toasted peanuts or 4 tablespoons peanut butter
1 tablespoon tomato purée
2 tablespoons tomato ketchup
150ml (5 fl oz) tinned coconut milk
1 teaspoon dark brown sugar

1 teaspoon fish sauce (page 36)
4 tablespoons vegetable oil
1 batch Panaeng curry paste (*page 138*)
150ml (5 fl oz) chicken stock or water
1 stalk lemon grass, cross-cut (*page 30*)
2 or 3 lime leaves, shredded
4 tablespoons chopped holy (or purple) basil leaves

GARNISH

some whole toasted peanuts
some red bell pepper slices
some red chilli slices

1 Divest the meat of any unwanted matter and cut it into 3cm cubes.
2 Preheat the oven to 190°C/375°F/Gas 5.
3 Put the peanuts, tomato purée and ketchup, coconut milk, sugar and fish sauce into the blender – to achieve a thick purée using a little water as necessary.
4 Heat the oil in the wok. Stir-fry the curry paste for about one minute.
5 Add the meat cubes and briskly stir-fry for about 3 minutes.
6 Put the stock, purée, lemon grass and lime leaves into a 2.75 litre casserole pot and put it, lid on, into the oven.
7 After 20 minutes, inspect and stir. It should be beginning to dry up.
8 After 15 minutes, inspect again. It will be reasonably thick and dry now, so add enough water to keep it mobile.
9 Repeat stage 8 after 15 more minutes, this time stirring in the fresh leaves.
10 Remove the pot after a further 10 minutes. It has now had an hour in the oven, and the meat should be nicely tender (if not, carry on casseroling), the gravy fairly thick. Salt to taste. Garnish and serve.

KHAENG MYANMAR PED
Burmese-Style Duck Curry

Chiang Mai is Thailand's northern-most province. Although it shares its border with Burma there is no official passage between the two countries. There's little reason for the tourist to visit here, although there is beautiful wild countryside. There is also the fascinating elephant training camp for young elephants near Mae Taeng, as an all year round alternative to Surin's November elephant round up festival.

More alluringly, there's Burma so close, yet inaccessible over the border. Few tourists visit the town of Ban Thaton. Even Thais call it 'world's end'. But if you do ever want a wonderful few moments of tranquillity, stay at the River Lodge Hotel, which is on the Mae Nam Kok river. Here amongst palms, peace and hill tribes, you can wish for few better places for the world to end.

This recipe uses a river duck, curried Burmese-style. It uses plentiful turmeric, chilli and galangal and is based, chef told me, on a dish he frequently has when he pops over the border to call on his friends and relatives. In Burma, this dish is called Bairthar Hin.

SERVES: 4

700g (1½lb) skinned duck breast
6 cloves, garlic
5cm cube of ginger or galangal
2cm cube of turmeric root (if available)
8 tablespoons crispy fried onion (*page 48*)
4 tablespoons vegetable oil

1 teaspoon shrimp paste (*page 36*)
1 teaspoon fish sauce (*page 36*)
1 tablespoon tomato purée
1 tablespoon tamarind purée (*page 47*)
200ml chicken stock or water (*page 43*)
2 tablespoons very finely chopped fresh coriander
4 tinned tomatoes

salt to taste

SPICES

1 teaspoon powdered turmeric
1 teaspoon chilli powder
1 teaspoon coriander powder
½ teaspoon cummin powder

---

1   Grind the garlic, ginger, turmeric root and onion in the blender, using just enough water to achieve a thickish paste.
2   Cut the duck breast into bite-sized pieces, and put into a non-metallic mixing bowl.
3   Add the paste and work it well into the duck. Cover and refrigerate the bowl for at least 12 hours.
4   To cook, preheat the oven to 190°C/375°F/Gas 5.
5   Heat the oil in the wok. Stir-fry the spices for 30 seconds. Add the shrimp paste and stir-fry for 30 seconds more. Add the duck with all the marinade and briskly stir-fry for about 3 minutes.
6   Transfer to a 2.75 litre lidded casserole with the fish sauce, tomato and tamarind purées and the stock. Put the pot into the oven.
7   Remove after 25 minutes. Stir well, adding the remaining ingredients. Return to the oven.
8   Remove after 25 to 30 minutes more. Salt to taste.
9   Serve with rice.

PEPPER ON VINE

CHAPTER 10

RICE

Rice is so important in Thailand, that the summons to the table is *kin khao* (literally 'eat rice'). Equally, the main Thai greeting, for which we'd say 'how are you?' literally translates as 'have you eaten (rice)?' Since wheat is scarcely grown in Thailand, rice is the country's major staple, being used either in noodle form (see Chapter 11) or as rice.

No meal is complete without rice. Every Thai eats about 500g (1 lb) of rice a day. The favourite breakfast is Khao Tom (*page 75*) – or Conjee – boiled rice with shredded pork, shrimp, egg, chicken or meat, or preserved fish and pickles. Rice is mandatory at other meals. A large bowl is always the centre-piece at lunch or dinner. Other dishes surround it.

There are two rice types: glutinous or sticky, the favourite of north Thailand, and fluffy rice, popular everywhere. Some fluffy varieties are expensive : but jasmine fragrant or basmati are the best to use.

A major variable in Thai rice is its age. It is best to keep grains for six months to one year. At that age it is dry, opaque and dusty, needing a little more water when cooking, but it is better for stir-fries. New crop is shinier but too soft, so goes stickier rather than fluffy. This is not to be confused with sticky rice, of either black or white varieties. I give recipes for these, but I have to say that, on the whole, Westerners prefer fluffy rice.

There is one further Thai rice item regarded as a delicacy. This is the crispy layer of rice which is deliberately created on the bottom of the pan. It is peeled off in large pieces, dried in the sun (after which it keeps), then fried in oil to make rice crackers or rice chips (*see page 70*), which are served with savoury peanut sauce or sweet syrup.

KHAO SUOY
Rice by Boiling

This is the quickest way to cook fluffy rice, and it can be ready to serve in just 15 minutes from the water boiling. Two factors are crucial for this method to work perfectly. Firstly, the rice must be basmati or jasmine fragrant rice. Other rices will require different timings and will have neither the same texture nor fragrance. Secondly, this is one of the few recipes in this book which requires precision timing. It is essential that for its few minutes on the boil, you concentrate on it, or else it may overcook and become stodgy. The pandanus leaf is (like bay leaf) a flavouring option. A small portion of dry rice per person is 225g (8oz) – large is 350g (12oz).

SERVES: 4

225g to 350g (8 to 12oz) basmati rice
1.2 to 1.75 litres (2 to 3 pints) water
5cm (2 inch) piece of pandanus leaf

1   Pick through the rice to remove grit and impurities.
2   Boil the water. It is not necessary to salt it. Chop up the pandanus leaf and add it into the water.
3   Whilst it is heating up, rinse the rice briskly with fresh cold water until most of the starch is washed out. Run boiling kettle water through the rice at the final rinse. This minimizes the temperature reduction of the boiling water when you put the rice into it.
4   When the water is boiling properly, put the rice into the pan. Start timing. Put the lid on the pan until the water comes back to the boil, then remove the lid. It takes 8 to 10 minutes from start to finish. Stir frequently.
5   After about 6 minutes, taste a few grains. As soon as the centre is no longer hard but still has a good al dente bite to it, drain off the water. The rice should seem slightly undercooked.
6   Shake off all excess water, then place the strainer on a dry tea towel which will help remove the last of the water.
7   After a minute, place the rice in a warmed serving dish. You can serve it now or, preferably, put it into a very low oven or warming drawer for at least 30 minutes. As it dries, the grains will separate and become fluffy. It can be held in the warmer for up to 90 minutes. Or it can be cooked and reheated in a wok (quickly stir-fry without any oil).

KHAO PLAO
Rice by Absorption

Cooking rice in a pre-measured ratio of water which is all absorbed into the rice is undoubtedly the best way to do it. Provided that you use basmati rice, the finished grains are longer, thinner and much more fragrant and flavoured than they are after boiling.

It's useful to know that 300g (10oz) is 2 tea cups of dry rice, and 600ml (20 fl oz) is about 1⅓ volume of water to 1 of rice. This 1:2 ratio is easy to remember, but do step up or step down the quantities as required in proportion. For small appetites, for instance, use 225g rice to 450ml water (8oz to 16 fl oz) to serve four people. For large appetites use 350g rice : 700ml.

Cooking rice does need some practice, but after a few goes at it you'll do it without thinking. Here is my foolproof method.

300g (10oz) basmati rice
600ml (20 fl oz) water

---

1   Soak the rice in water to cover for about half an hour.
2   Rinse it until the water runs more or less clear, then drain.
3   Bring the measured water to the boil in a saucepan (as heavy as possible, and with a lid) or casserole dish with a capacity at least twice the volume of the drained rice.
4   As soon as it is boiling add the rice and stir in well.
5   As soon as it starts bubbling put the lid on the pan and reduce the heat to under half. Leave well alone for 8 minutes.
6   Inspect. Has the liquid on top been absorbed? If not, replace the lid and leave for 2 minutes. If and when it has, stir the rice well, ensuring that it is not sticking to the bottom. Now taste. It should not be brittle in the middle. If it is, add a little more water and return to the heat.
7   Place the saucepan or casserole into a warming drawer or oven pre-heated to its lowest setting. This should be no lower than 80°C/175°F and no higher than 100°C/210°F/Gas 1/8. You can serve the rice at once, but the longer you leave it, the more separate the grains will be. Thirty minutes is fine, but it will be quite safe and happy left for up to 90 minutes.

KKHAO NIAW DAENG
Black Glutinous Rice

This variety of rice must not be confused with American wild rice. Thai black rice is a glutinous variety, readily available from Thai shops. Its grains are shorter than jasmine fragrant rice but longer than white glutinous rice. The colour of the grain varies from pale buff to dark burnt coffee. It looks as though it has been roasted, but Thai black rice is naturally this colour. It is widely used in Thai desserts (see Chapter 13) and is generally cooked by soaking and steaming to produce sticky rice.

It may well be untraditional, but I prefer to cook this rice so that its grains are separate. This is best done by boiling (see page 150). The extraordinary phenomenon here is that before long the water goes purply-pink.

The outcome of boiling white and black rice together is very pretty. Here the black rice is fully cooked on its own and the water drained, the result is a deep reddy-brown rice with a delicious firm nutty texture.

SERVES: 4

225g to 350g (8oz to 12oz) Thai black glutinous rice
1.2 to 1.75 litres (2 to 3 pints) water

1   Pick through the rice to remove grit and impurities.
2   Soak the rice for an hour, then rinse it with a few changes of cold water.
3   Boil the water and follow the recipe on page 150 from its stage 2 to its end.

CHEF'S TIP: *As this rice has its husks still on it will take longer to cook than rice without husks.*

KHAO PA-SOM
Black and White Rice

Again, it is not traditional to mix black and white rice (except for desserts) but it is really superb in appearance, and the taste and texture are equally superb.

To prevent the white rice going pink, the black and white rices must be cooked separately then mixed prior to serving. Mix cooked white rice from the recipe on pages 150 or 151 and black rice from the previous recipe.

KHAO NIAW
Sticky Rice

Glutinous or sticky rice, called *khao niaw*, is grown in the Issan hill district of north Thailand, and is a shorter, fatter grain than fluffy rice. It is cheaper and the locals say it is more filling. To achieve a sticky texture, so sticky that you can squeeze the cooked rice into a ball, the way the northerners like it, requires a long soak of at least six hours, preferably twelve. This totally saturates and softens the grains.

The rice is then transferred to a moist cloth which is put into a purpose-made hat-shaped basket which is placed over a water-filled clay pot. The rice is then steamed for half an hour. Here this is simulated using a saucepan, clean tea towel and a strainer.

SERVES: 4

225g to 350g (8oz to 12oz) Thai glutinous white rice
1.5 to 2 litres (2 to 3 pints) water

1   Soak the rice for at least six hours. Drain it and rinse it several times.
2   Bring the water to the simmer. Using a large enough strainer, line it with a clean white tea towel. Put the rice in and the strainer over the saucepan. It must not touch the water.
3   Put the lid on and steam the rice for about 30 minutes. Inspect from time to time to ensure there is ample water.
4   To serve, scrape the rice off the tea towel and place it in a bowl.

KHAO PAD
Basic Thai Fried Rice

Khao Pad simply means 'fried rice', and it is eaten at any time in Thailand from breakfast to bed time. Unflavoured rice is rarely eaten (except by the sick and infirm). But you do need one of the recipes given earlier in this chapter to create fried rice.

Absolutely any ingredient can be incorporated with Khao Pad – chicken, meat, seafood, vegetables, herbs, fruit, etc.

Here is my basic recipe for fried rice, which is tasty enough to be eaten as it is with your meal. I have then given a number of variations for you to try. These are simply examples and you can invent your own combinations, too.

KHAO PAD TAMADA
Ordinary Fried Rice

1 batch rice cooked by either of the methods on pages 150 or 151
2 tablespoons sesame, sunflower or soy oil
1 or 2 cloves garlic (optional) finely chopped
4 tablespoons spring onion leaves
1 stalk lemon grass cross-cut (*page 30*)
1 teaspoon fish sauce (*page 36*)
½ teaspoon sugar (optional)

1   Heat the oil in the wok. Stir-fry the garlic, onion and lemon grass for about 30 seconds.
2   Add about half the rice (which can be hot or cold), briskly stir-frying it to mix it. Add the remaining rice and, when sizzling, the fish sauce and sugar.
3   Stir it in well, and serve when it is hot right through.

Add the items below at the end of stage 2.

KHAO PAD NUA
Beef Fried Rice

Add 140g (5oz) fried rump steak strips

KHAO PAD MOO
Pork Fried Rice

Add 140g (5oz) fried pork strips

KHAO PAD KAI
Egg Fried Rice

Add 2 eggs scrambled or omletted

KHAO PAD GUNG
Prawn Fried Rice

Add cooked peeled prawns or king prawns

KHAO PAD SUPPAROT
Pineapple Fried Rice

Add some pineapple chunks

KHAO PAD HORAPA
Basil Fried Rice

Add some chopped holy basil leaves

KHAO PAD MAPRAO
Coconut Fried Rice

Add some fresh grated coconut

KHAO PAD NAM PRIG
Chilli Fried Rice

Add some chopped red and/or green chillies

KHAO YAM
Rice Salad

From southern Thailand comes this delightful salad. It is served cold, and it's up to you what ingredients you add to your rice. Here is my example.

SERVES: 4

1 batch rice cooked by either of the methods on pages 150 or 151

1 tablespoon sesame or sunflower oil

3 tablespoons cooked sweet-corn kernels

1 tablespoon strips of red bell pepper

1 or 2 green chillies, cross-cut (optional)

2 tablespoons crispy fried onion (*page 48*)

1 teaspoon lemon grass, finely cross-cut (*page 30*)

1 teaspoon fish sauce (*page 36*)

GARNISH

**some of the above items
plus a sprig of basil
some 'ribbed' cucumber slices**

1   Mix everything together.
2   Garnish and serve cold.

LEMON GRASS

CHAPTER 11

NOODLES

K*UAYTIAW*, (pronounced git-dtee-oh), is the general Thai word for noodles. They are all made from a flour dough, which is cut or extended into strips of varying thickness. Which flour is used determines the type of noodle. The three types used in Chinese cuisine are rice flour, wheat flour and mung bean flour. They all start life from a sheet rolled out from the dough. Rice noodles are the most prolific.

The noodle is named according to its thickness. *Kuaytiaw sen yai* is wide at around 2cm to 3cm per strip. *Sen lek* (or rice sticks) is narrow at 5mm per strip, and *sen mee* is thin at 1 to 2mm. A further rice noodle is the wiry very thin variety which resembles white birds' nests. Also called rice vermicelli noodles, these are known in Thai as *kuaytiaw jeen*.

Wheat noodle dough always contains egg yolk which gives rise to its name egg noodle – *kuaytiaw – ba mee* in Thai. These are about 2mm thick and are usually relatively straight but can be produced in a lightly curled form. Mung bean noodles (*kuaytiaw wun-sen*) are very thin thread-like hard noodles (*see page 162*), called glass or cellophane noodles.

Some noodles are available fresh (or you can make your own – see page 165). All are available dried in packets and they just need reconstituting. The thinnest noodles can be deep-fried to create a gorgeous crispy texture (*see page 164*). All noodles can be reconstituted in water, though unlike pasta (spaghetti in particular) they don't need prolonged boiling.

PAD THAI
Thai Stir-Fried Noodles (national dish) or Dragon Fry

Of all the famous Thai dishes, Pad Thai has to be the most prolific. You'll see it everywhere you go in Thailand. It is easy to cook, and has the simplest name – Thai Stir-Fry. It is a noodle dish to which almost anything can be added according to your taste. It is indeed a national dish.

At its simplest, it is available from street hawkers who carry their kit on two baskets suspended from a yoke which balances on their shoulders. One basket contains a lighted charcoal fire above which bubbles a pan of boiling water. The other basket has all their raw ingredients. Noodles, prawns, beef, chicken, tofu, eggs, vegetables, herbs and garnishes. Pad Thai is also available from kiosks, cafés and the smartest restaurants. Wherever you go on the streets, you'll see well-dressed office workers and shop assistants queuing for their Pad Thai, for their early hours breakfast to last thing bedtime snack, and gobbling down the contents of their bowl with chopsticks and Chinese spoon. You'll pay pennies for it from the hawkers and pounds for the same dish at exclusive restaurants.

It traditionally uses *sen lek* (small rice noodles), but *ba-mee* (egg noodles) are equally acceptable.

This dish was given a spirited name by a charming Korean friend of mine, Yungoo Rhee, when her PR company, aptly called 'Oriental Matters', set about working for Blue Dragon. She called the dish Dragon Fry.

SERVES: 4

110g (4oz) dried egg noodles
3 tablespoons sunflower or
 soya oil
2 cloves garlic, very finely
 chopped
3cm cube of ginger, shredded
1 teaspoon red curry paste
 (*page 137*)
1 teaspoon chilli sauce
 (*page 169*)
1 teaspoon oyster sauce
200ml (7 fl oz) stock or water
100g (3½oz) skinned chicken
 breast

100g (3½oz) lean pork
8 cooked king prawns
20 to 30 dried prawns
 (reconstituted in water)
1 tablespoon chopped red bell
 peppers
1 or more red chillies, chopped
2 or 3 tablespoons beansprouts
3 tablespoons chopped spring
 onions, leaves only
2 tablespoons chopped basil
1 tablespoon chopped coriander
sweet soy and/or fish sauce to
 season

--- GARNISH ---

spring onion tassels	spring onion leaves in long shreds
chilli tassels	toasted peanuts
	lime wedges

1   Cut the chicken and pork into 4cm x 2cm x 3mm strips.

2   Bring a litre of water to the boil in a 2.25 litre saucepan.

3   Break up the noodles a little, as you add them to the saucepan, and move them around to help them break up.

4   Take the pan off the heat and put it to one side.

5   Heat the oil in the wok. Stir-fry the garlic, ginger, red curry paste and chilli and oyster sauce for 30 seconds.

6   Add the stock or water and when it is simmering, add the chicken and pork. Stir-fry for about 3 minutes. Add the prawns and continue simmering for a further 3 minutes.

7   Add the remaining ingredients.

8   When this is simmering, drain the noodles and add them to the wok.

9   Season with soy and fish sauce.

10   Garnish and serve.

FACING PREVIOUS PAGE   Clockwise from the top: Fragrant Jasmine Rice, gushing from its strainer basket (page 149), Black Glutinous Rice (page 152), Chilli in Fish Sauce (page 36), Cucumber Chutney (page 174) and in the traditional cooking pot Moslem-style curry with Oyster Mushrooms and Prawns. (page 144). Note the Pandanus Leaves (pages 32 and 56) and Cassia Bark.

FACING PAGE   Thailand's celebrated national dish – Pad Thai (page 158). A meal in itself, it always contains noodles, and here it also has King Prawn, Chicken and Beef.
Note in the background: bottled Fish Sauce (page 36), a special Thai Paste (story page 42) and the coconut scraper.

KHAI-SOI LAMPANG
Northern Style Curried Noodles

At the time of the British Raj, when Burma was part of the Empire, a vast trade took place in teak. In those days the border into Thailand was open and the ancient northern temple Thai town of Lampang became a teak trade centre. It still retains teak buildings and a relaxed provincial charm. It also gained notoriety because, the story goes, the venerated Emerald Buddha statue (actually made from jade) was being transported to a royal palace in the 16th century. However, the elephant in charge of transport apparently refused to move the tiny 0.6 metre high statue beyond Lampang. It stayed there for some time before being taken to the royal chapel at Bangkok's Grand Palace, where it now resides.

Lampang's other legacies include pony-trap taxis, curried noodles and plentiful noodle shops. This dish, closely resembling Burma's national noodle dish, *Kaushwe-Kyaw*, is rather different from normal Thai flavours.

You can garnish this with the indigenous fruit of Lampang, the longan, a berry available from Thai shops, when in season.

110g (4oz) egg noodles
100g (3½oz) skinned chicken breast, shredded
100g (3½oz) tiniest cooked baby shrimps, shell-on
3 tablespoons sesame oil
1 teaspoon 'magic paste' (*page 42*)

1 stalk lemon grass cross-cut (*page 30*)
2 teaspoons *nam pla prig* (*page 170*)
2 tablespoons spring onion leaves, cross-cut
2 tablespoons chopped coriander leaves
1 tablespoon chopped mint leaves
salt to taste

--- SPICES ---

½ teaspoon turmeric
½ teaspoon ground coriander

½ teaspoon ground cummin
½ teaspoon chilli powder
½ teaspoon white pepper

--- GARNISH ---

some red pepper slices
some freshly ground black pepper
some lime wedges

---

1 Put the noodles into a saucepan of boiling water and turn off the heat. After a couple of minutes, stir and carefully loosen the noodles. Repeat a few minutes later by which time they will be fully softened.

2 Heat the oil and stir-fry the 'magic paste' for about 30 seconds. Add the spices and 3 tablespoons of water and stir-fry for a further minute.

3 Add the chicken and the shrimps and continue to stir-fry for 5 minutes, adding just enough water to keep things mobile.

4 Mix in the lemon grass, the *nam pla prig* and the leaves.

5 Drain the (hot) noodles and add them into the wok.

6. Stir-fry until the chicken is fully cooked. Salt to taste.

7 Garnish and serve.

CORIANDER

YAM KUAYTIAW SEN MEE
Rice Noodles Salad with King Prawn, Mango and Orange

This is a very colourful salad using flat medium-sized rice noodles (*sen lek see page 157*). They should have a satisfying al dente texture, and they work exceptionally well served cold in a salad. The fruit, in this case orange wedges, adds to the glamour, as you can see in the picture on the cover.

SERVES: 4

110g (4oz) *sen lek* rice noodles
1 tablespoon sunflower or soya oil
2 tablespoons chopped spring onion leaves and bulbs
2 tablespoons chopped coriander leaves

1 tablespoon chopped mint leaves
8 cooked, peeled king prawns
2 tablespoons freshly squeezed lime juice
1 tablespoon freshly squeezed orange juice
salt to taste

GARNISH

some orange wedges, pith removed
red and/or green chilli tassels
some crispy fried garlic and/or onion (*pages 45 and 48*)

1   Soak the noodles at room temperature for 15 to 20 minutes then check that they are softened then drain them.
2   Add the remaining ingredients, mixing them well in. Salt to taste.
3   Garnish and serve cold.

WUN-SEN PAD TAENG-KWA KRATEN

Glass Noodles Stir-Fried with Cucumber and Pickled Garlic

Glass noodles (*wun sen*) are, as described on page 157, made from soya beans. They are only available dried, not fresh, and resemble thinly spun fibre-glass in colour, texture and taste too, when raw. They are hard to eat raw and hard to break. Once softened they are very palatable, becoming clear, hence their name glass or cellophane noodles. In Thailand, they appear in salads, and soups or as a spring roll stuffing. Another favourite is casseroled with prawns. Here they are stir-fried with optional minced pork, cucumber and pickled garlic.

SERVES: 4

- 80g (3oz) *wun-sen* glass noodles
- 2 tablespoons sunflower or soya oil
- 1 teaspoon shrimp paste (*page 36*)
- 4 tablespoons, very finely chopped onion
- 6 tablespoons coconut milk
- 250ml (9 fl oz) fish stock or water (*page 44*)
- 1 teaspoon fish sauce
- 100g (3½oz) cooked minced pork (optional)
- 1 tablespoon chopped red bell peppers
- 10cm pieces cucumber, cut into small cubes
- 1 teaspoon soy sauce
- 3 or 4 cloves pickled garlic, chopped (*page 173*)

GARNISH

some finely chopped coriander and/or manglak basil leaves

1   Use kitchen scissors to cut off the amount of noodles you wish to use.
2   Soak them in warm water for 15 to 20 minutes, until they are translucent and soft.
3   During stage 2, heat the oil in the wok. Stir-fry the shrimp paste for 30 seconds. Add the onion and stir-fry for 30 more seconds.
4   Stir in the stock and fish sauce, and when simmering add the cooked pork and peppers.
5   When again simmering, drain the noodles and add them to the wok. Stir until warm then add the cucumber, soy, pickled garlic and once hot, garnish and serve.

MEE GROB
Crispy Fried Noodles with a Sweet Sauce

Mee Grob (pronounced *krob*), means literally 'noodles crispy'. This typical Thai shorthand so much understates the outstanding qualities of this dish, that it is easy to pass over it on the Thai restaurant menu. But it is nearly always there – and Thais know how good it is. It's another national dish.

Professional Thai chefs soak the noodles then deep-fry them, claiming crispier results. This method is, frankly, really dangerous, adding the water to the hot oil makes it become explosive. My method is to use the noodles dry. When fried, they whoosh up quickly in the oil, but do not splutter, and if left for a while, they became perfectly crisp.

The sauce is poured over the noodles. Serve it as a crunchy, tasty side dish.

SERVES: 4
---

6 tablespoons sunflower or
　soya oil
50g (1¾oz) palm or brown
　sugar
1 teaspoon fish sauce (*page 36*)
2 tablespoons rice vinegar
150ml (5 fl oz) water
2 cloves garlic, chopped

110g (4oz) spring onion
　leaves and bulbs, finely chopped
2 teaspoons (or more) chilli jam
　(*page 169*)
20 to 24 dried prawns, reconstituted
　in water and drained (optional)
oil for deep-frying
250g (9oz) wiry rice noodles (*sen-mee*)

GARNISH
---

some chopped spring onion
some red pepper shreds

1　Heat the sunflower or soya oil in the wok. Carefully add the sugar, fish sauce, vinegar and water to the wok (it will splutter if the oil is too hot). Then increase the heat whilst stir-frying for about 5 minutes.

2　Add the garlic, spring onions, chilli, and the prawns, and stir-fry for a further 2 minutes. You should now have a fairly glutinous syrupy texture. Take off the heat.

3　Heat the deep-fryer to 190°C. Split the noodles into 3 or 4 bundles. Carefully put the first bundle into the deep fryer. It will whoosh up and swell. Once the sizzling stops (in less than a minute), remove it and drain. Cook the remaining noodles in the same way.

4　Prior to serving, reheat the sauce in the wok. Pour the sauce over the noodles. Garnish and serve at once.

KUAYTIAW LOT
Steamed Rice Noodle Spring Roll

These are like spring rolls except that the wrapping is a noodle sheet and the cooking is by steaming. The stuffing can be any of the variations on pages 50 and 51. The rice sheets can be purchased ready to use at the Thai shop, where they are called *sen yai neung*.

MAKES: 4 ROLLS

1 batch rice noodle dough (*see below*)
4 tablespoons raw filling of your choice (*pages 50 and 51*)

1   Roll out the dough to a large thin square (2mm to 3mm) and cut it into 4 smaller squares which should be about 12 to 15cm per side.
2   Place one tablespoon of filling along the centre of a sheet. Fold and roll as shown in the drawing on page 63.
3   Place the rolls into the steamer basket and steam for about 8 to 10 minutes.

KUAY TIAW
Noodles

Making noodles yourself is actually very easy. You make a dough then either roll it out and cut into thin strips with the knife, or use a pasta-making machine. Professional noodle makers use neither device. They can make the thinnest strands simply by pulling the dough out by hand. If you ever get the chance to see it being done, don't miss it. Meanwhile, over the page is the technique for doing it at home.

MAKES: 250G (9OZ)

BA MEE
Egg Noodles

250g (9oz) plain flour
1 large egg yolk
1 tablespoon vegetable oil
1 teaspoon salt

1   Mix the flour with the egg, oil and salt, and just enough water for it to become a soft, sticky dough.
2   Either roll the dough out flat and cut strips as thinly as you can or use the pasta machine.

SEN YAI
Rice Noodle Sheet

250g (9oz) rice flour
1 tablespoon vegetable oil
1 teaspoon salt

Use the same method as for egg noodles (omitting the egg). Use the uncut sheet for the recipe on page 165.

Optionally you can incorporate finely chopped red and/or green chillies into the dough.

CHAPTER 12

ACCOMPANIMENTS

N O THAI MEAL or snack would be considered complete without a number of sauces, dips, chutneys and pickles. You'll often see a tray of four flavourings presented with the meal at restaurants in Thailand. These are sweet (straight sugar) salt, hot (chilli powder) and sour (tamarind). Other popular Thai flavours include factory-made ground dried fish or dried prawns. Such delights can be combined with any of the aforementioned four flavourings, especially with chilli. Next time you visit a Thai shop, search them out. There are a good many on offer. Also seek out bottled, vinegared pickled vegetables. In addition, you'll now find a wide range of Thai ingredients available from good supermarkets, such as Tesco.

On pages 173 and 174 I give six such recipes if you prefer to make your own, and they are easy to make. The other recipes are all equally easy and include five chilli recipes, two tamarind recipes, the celebrated satay dip, a 'sour' soy dip and, quickest of all, I think, cucumber chutney which literally takes but seconds.

NAM PRIG
Hot Chilli

It's chillies with everything in Thailand. If you are able to visit a Thai shop, you'll find they stock tiny red and green fresh chillies – *prig kee noo*, mentioned on page 33. Failing these, use red cayennes (as used in Indian cooking), *Nam* means liquid, *prig* means chilli and this sauce, because it is vinegar based, lasts indefinitely. It matures with age. Use it with virtually any savoury dish.

MAKES: ABOUT 350G (12OZ)

225g (8oz) tiny Thai red cayenne chillies
6 cloves garlic, very finely chopped

75ml (2½ fl oz) distilled white vinegar
50ml (2 fl oz) bottled lemon juice
2 tablespoons fish sauce (*page 36*)
25ml (1 fl oz) water

---

1   De-stalk the chillies. Put everything into the blender and mulch down to a purée.
2   Pour into sterilized jar(s).

AUBERGINE

NAM PRIG DAENG
Red Chilli Sauce

This chilli sauce is cooked first. It is oven roasted then ground. Make a large batch which saves on smells and washing up. It will not preserve beyond a few days, however, so use the ice-cube mould and the freezer (see pages 22-4) to keep the surplus. Silicha brand is Thailand's most popular bottled chilli sauce. Made in Silicha, a district near Pataya which specializes in the manufacturing of chilli sauces, it is available from Thai shops.

—————— MAKES: ABOUT 310G (11OZ) SAUCE ——————

20 cloves garlic, whole but peeled	1 tablespoon palm or brown sugar
225g (8oz) onion, quartered	60g (2oz) dried prawns
12 to 20 fresh red cayenne chillies	4 tablespoons sunflower or soy oil
	2 tablespoons fish sauce (*page 36*)
	2 teaspoons salt

1   Put the garlic, onion and chillies into the oven preheated to 180°C and bake for about 30 minutes.
2   Allow to cool then put them into the food processor, with the remaining ingredients and pulse down to a thick paste, using just enough water to achieve it.
3   Freeze the surplus, as described above.

NAM PRIG KAPEE
Chilli with Shrimp Paste

This is Thailand's favourite hot sauce, containing her two favourite ingredients: chilli (*prig*) and shrimp paste (*kapee*). Here I'm using some of the *nam prig* from page 12/1. It keeps indefinitely.

—————— MAKES: ABOUT 100G (3½OZ) ——————

90g (3oz) *nam prig* (hot chilli) (*page 169*)
1 teaspoon shrimp paste (*page 36*)
1 teaspoon 'magic' paste (page 42)

1   Mix everything well.
2   Pour into sterilized jar(s).

NAM PRIG PAD
Chilli Jam

This is a particularly tasty chilli syrup. Thais would use the ubiquitous fish sauce/shrimp paste combination in this, but I've called them optional, so that this sauce rings the changes. It will keep indefinitely.

─────── MAKES: ABOUT 350ML (12 FL OZ) ───────

6 to 12 fresh red cayenne chillies	(optional *page 36*)
225g (8oz) castor sugar	1 teaspoon fish sauce (optional *page 36*)
1/2 teaspoon shrimp paste	2 teaspoons salt

1   Mash the chillies down as finely as you can in a blender using just enough water to achieve it.
2   Boil 300ml (10 fl oz) water. Add the sugar, chilli mash and simmer until you get a thickish paste.
3   Add the salt. It should still be pourable when cold. If it isn't, add a little water. Pour into sterilized bottles.

NAM PLA PRIG
Chilli in Fish Sauce

Thailand is favourite, ubiquitous accompaniment. Simple to make. Keeps in the fridge for a week, but will freeze. Note the traditional number of chillies.

─────── MAKES: 100ML (3 FL OZ) SAUCE ───────

60ml (2 fl oz) fish sauce (*page 36*)	21 Thai *prig kee noo* chillies (*page 33*) red and green or 5 cayenne chillies
40ml (1½ fl oz) water	

1   Mix the sauce with the water in a bowl. Cross-cut the chillies into the thinnest possible rings. Put them, seeds and all, into the bowl. Ready to serve.

NAM PRIG MAK-KAM
Hot Tamarind Sauce

Hot and sour is what this sauce is. As with the previous recipe, you use some of the *nam prig* from page 168 to which you add tamarind. It will keep indefinitely.

—— MAKES: ABOUT 235G (8OZ) ——

175g (6oz) *nam prig* (hot chilli) (*page 169*)
60g (2oz) tamarind purée (*page 47*)

1 Mix everything well.
2 Pour into sterilized jar(s).

NAM MAK-KAM PAK-CHEE
Tamarind and Coriander Dip

This delightful combination of sour from the tamarind and musky from the coriander is quite superb, if a bit of an acquired taste. Since this does not keep beyond a few days in the fridge, this recipe makes a small batch.

—— MAKES: ABOUT 100G (3½OZ) ——

2 tablespoons tamarind purée (*page 47*)
2 teaspoons 'magic paste' (*page 42*)
50ml (2 fl oz) water
1 teaspoon salt

1 Mix everything together well.
2 Chill and serve.

NAM JIM SATAY
Satay Peanut Dip

Goes with satay (*see page 59*) like love and marriage or a horse and carriage – but it is equally good accompanying other starters from Chapter 2. This version of satay sauce uses peanut butter and saves you a great deal of time grinding fresh peanuts to a paste.

MAKES: ABOUT 160G (5½OZ) SAUCE

4 tablespoons vegetable oil
1 teaspoon 'magic paste'
 (*page 42*)
6 tablespoons smooth peanut
butter

4 tablespoons thick coconut milk
2 teaspoons soy sauce
1 teaspoon fish sauce (*page 36*)
1 teaspoon chilli sauce
 (*page 169*)

1 Heat the oil in the wok. Stir-fry the 'magic paste' for 30 seconds.
2 Add the remaining ingredients and briskly stir-fry the mixture for a couple of minutes, adding just enough water to keep it thick but pourable.
3 Serve hot or cold.

NAM JIM SIIYU
Sour Soy Sauce

So simple, so effective as a dip with crispy items. It keeps indefinitely, so if you like it, make up a large batch.

MAKES: 150ML (¼ PINT) SAUCE

60ml (2 fl oz) dark soy sauce
80ml (3 fl oz) rice vinegar
1 tablespoon palm or brown sugar
1 teaspoon salt

1 Mix everything together.
2 Pour into sterilized bottles.

MANAU DONG
Pickled Lime

Thai food has a wonderful balance of sweetness, heat and fragrance. This tart pickle provides the ideal contrast to the palate. It's easy to make, lasts indefinitely and is delicious. Here I give the method for Manau Dong – pickled lime.

───────── MAKES: AMPLE PICKLE ─────────

12 limes	400ml (13 fl oz) water
300ml (½ pint) rice wine	1 tablespoon salt
300ml (½ pint) rice vinegar	1 tablespoon sugar

1   Bring the vinegar and water to the simmer. Add the limes and turn off the heat. Add the salt and sugar.
2   When it is cool put it into suitable sterilized lidded jars. Top up with vinegar/water mixture if needed.
3   Leave it to mature for a month or two then use as required.

PAK DONG
Pickled Mixed Vegetables

500g (18oz) mixed, prepared raw vegetables (choose from cauliflower, carrot, shallots, baby corn, white cabbage, etc.)
remaining ingredients and method as pickled limes, above

KRATHIEM DONG
Pickled Garlic

40 to 50 plump peeled garlic cloves
remaining ingredients and method as pickled limes, above

KIAMCHAI DONG
Pickled Mustard Leaf

A particular Thai speciality. It is simply leaf in brine. Also called mustard cabbage, it is sometimes available fresh in Thai shops (or Chinese shops as *dai gai choi*). Alternatively look and ask for this one ready bottled in Thai shops.

MAMUANG DONG
Pickled Mango

4 or 5 peeled, pitted sour mangoes
remaining ingredients and method as pickled limes, above

PRIG DONG
Pickled Chillies

250g (9oz) cayenne or Thai chillies, de-stalked
remaining ingredients and method as pickled limes, above

TAENG-KWA YAM
Cucumber Chutney

This is a refreshing chutney, and it takes but seconds to make. Serve it at once or else it discolours quickly.

MAKES: ENOUGH FOR 4 PEOPLE

15cm cucumber	2 teaspoons sweet soy sauce
2 tablespoons chopped red bell pepper	6 tablespoons wine vinegar
	½ teaspoon salt
1 or 2 green chillies, chopped	1 tablespoon palm or brown sugar

1   Peel the cucumber, cutting it into rectangular shape. Cut it into 5mm cubes. Cut the red pepper into 0.5cm squares.
2   Mix the chilli, soy, vinegar, salt and sugar together in a bowl.
3   Just prior to serving, add the cucumber and pepper, stir and serve.

VEGETABLE CARVING

VEGETABLE CARVING is an art form which was developed in the Thai royal kitchens centuries ago to garnish the court food. Originally, real flowers were used. It still is a Thai tradition, as can be seen with the orchids in some of the pictures in this book. When real flowers were out of season it must have occurred to an artistic royal chef that vegetables could be carved to represent flowers. Food dyes transformed white radishes into elaborate purple orchids.

Vegetable carving became a kitchen specification, and soon the most elaborate carvings were the result. Using virtually any vegetable or fruit, and creating not only all types of flower, but a huge range of still-lifes, nets, baskets, fish, animals and birds.

The method and the results follow the ancient traditions, and it takes years of apprenticeship to become expert. Some complex examples are shown in some of the photographs in this book. They were kindly supplied by the restaurant nominated as Britian's number one Thai by my *Good Curry Guide*, London's Blue Elephant.

If you feel inclined, you could experiment with such carving by copying the pictures. You'll need a sharp knife, small carver, plenty of patience and lots of practice. The results are rewarding and the carvings will keep covered with a damp cloth in the fridge for a day or two.

A really foolproof method of making pretty little garnishes is by using the tiniest marzipan/confectionery cutters. Available at cookshops, they come in all sorts of shapes – hearts, fish, animals, diamond, etc.

I've given some methods for simpler garnishes, such as chilli or spring onion tassels, tomato roses, white radish daisy and for fun, how about a cucumber and carrot frog!

CHILLI OR SPRING ONION TASSELS

Tassels are really easy to make and are an attractive garnish that will make any dish look very professional and appetizing. To make a tassel you need a thin-walled vegetable with a thick top at one end and a hollow thin part at the other. Both chillies and spring onions are ideal candidates.

SPRING ONION TASSELS

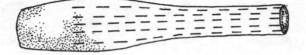

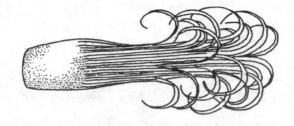

1   Peel away any discoloured greenery and then trim off enough of the green part to leave about 5cm attached to the white bulb. Trim off the hairy roots. Wash the spring onions well.

2   Using a small, sharp paring knife, make cuts down the length of the green, away from the bulb, leaving most of the bulb uncut. Turn the onion round a little and repeat the cutting process until all the green part is cut into 1mm threads.

3   Immerse the onions in a bowl of iced water and leave in the fridge for between 2 and 24 hours. The effect of the chilled water is to tighten the structure which causes the threads to curl backwards.

CHILLI TASSELS

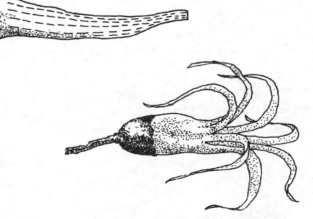

1   Wash the chillies but leave the stalks on. Snip off the tip.
2   Cut down the length of the chilli, with a pair of sharp nail scissors, leaving 1/6 of the chilli uncut at the stalk end. Using the scissors, remove any pith and discard with the seeds.
3   Immerse in a bowl of iced water and leave in the fridge for between 2 and 24 hours.

WHITE RADISH DAISY

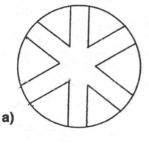

a)

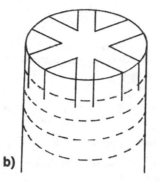

b)

c)

1   To make, say, 12 daisies you need a peeled white radish (mooli) cut to a cylinder 4cm diameter by about 12cm long.
2   Using a really sharp paring knife or safety razor blade, cut the 'petal' pattern on the top end of the mooli, about 1cm deep (a). Now cut the mooli cross-ways at about .75cm deep. The petal and 6 spare triangles will come free (b).
3   Repeat 11 more times.
4   Put a toothpick through the centre so that it just protrudes on one side of the petal.
5   Cut the carrot into thin slices and cut 12 circles about .5cm diameter (c).
5   Put the carrot on to the just protruding toothpick.
6   Place the daisy into a garlic chive stem or green drinking straw and arrange in a vase.

TOMATO ROSE

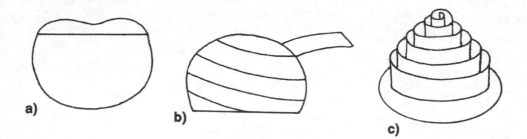

a)   b)   c)

1   Choose a firm, slightly underripe, tomato about 5cm in diameter. Remove the stalk and cut off the top to a point just under it (a).
2   Turn the tomato upside-down and using a very sharp paring knife or safety razor blade, start a cut about 3mm thick and 1.5cm wide.
3   Keeping this skin in one piece, work spirally downwards round the tomato until you have removed all the skin (b).
4   You now should have a long piece of skin and the centre of the tomato (which you can keep for some other use).
5   Roll the skin firmly round itself to create a spiral (c). Sit this on the slice you cut off in stage 1. Press it down and shape it like a rose.

CUCUMBER FROG

Bound to raise a smile is this little frog, made from cucumber and carrot. With a little ingenuity you could alternatively/also make mice, penguins, sharks, rabbits, etc.

---

cucumber
carrot

---

1   Take the end of the cucumber. Make a 30° cut at a point about 8cm down the cucumber, cutting up to about 6cm (a).
2   Sit the cucumber down on its diagonal end, and visualize your frog. Cut away a flat piece at the top for its face, and carry this down for its tummy (b).
3   Cut a small slit on each of its sides (to represent its knees and to hold its paws) (c).

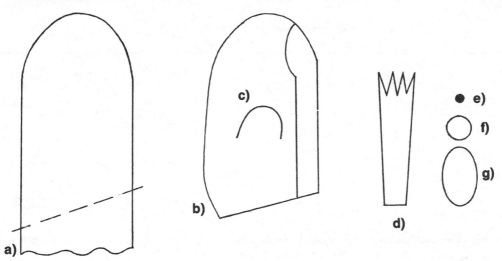

4   Cut 2 paws and 2 legs from spare cucumber, green side up (d). Cut
     the eyes' pupils from green cucumber (e).

5   Cut two eyes (f) and the tongue (g) from thin carrot. Fit the tongue
     into the face cutting a slit as required. Fix the carrot eyes using broken
     toothpicks, leaving a small amount protruding onto which you fit the
     green bit of the eye (f).

6   Wedge the paws into the slit and toothpick the legs underneath. And
     that's your frog (h).

CHAPTER 13

DESSERTS AND SWEET THINGS

A S WE HAVE seen, most Thai people do not eat their meals in courses. Everything, including sweet dishes, is served together. Maybe this is one reason why the Thai sweet dish repertoire is very limited. As we have also seen, Thai cooks usually add a little sugar to their savoury dishes. That, too, makes sweet dishes less important. Until recently, Thai households lacked ovens, and that fact, coupled with their scant use of dairy products, also helped restrict the range of desserts.

Fresh fruit (*polamai*) is universally popular with the full range of tropical items available at different times of year. Rice and bananas are the other major players on the Thai pudding menu. However, there are other relatively simple delights, and my selection here presents you with as wide a variety of choice as you need – from fritters to ice-cream and sugared nuts to sweet rice balls.

For want of a better place, I've ended up with lemon grass tea on page 189. It's absolutely gorgeous and very refreshing, and if I were you I'd make some now. It's a great way to end a Thai meal, too.

NAM TAN HIMAPHARN
Sugared Toasted Cashews

These nuts are superb to chew on at any time. Raw cashews (not salted ones) are either dry-fried or deep-fried (which is better) and sugared.

Make a large batch – they keep for months.

MAKES: 500G (18OZ) NUTS

500g (18oz) raw cashew nuts	50g (2oz) granulated sugar
600ml (1 pint) oil for deep-frying	50g (2oz) white rock sugar

1 Heat the oil in the wok.
2 Add the cashews, stirring all the time. As soon as they start going golden, turn off the heat and remove them from the oil and rest on kitchen paper.
3 Put them in a bowl. While they are still hot, mix them with most of the granulated sugar.
4 Let them cool, then add the remaining sugar.
5 Store in an air-tight tin.

KHAO NIAW MAN
Sticky Sweet Rice Balls

These marble-sized balls from northern Thailand are served cold. They are very easy to make, but you should use Thai glutinous rice so that they hold together. The rice is naturally white, but it is traditional to colour some of the balls with green, red and yellow (sometimes even blue and purple) food colouring. The only effective way to achieve this is to use tartrazine food colours. These can be omitted if you have an aversion to them.

Alternatively, you can use the Thai method of soaking the rice, which is to steep it in thin coconut milk for 4 hours.

SERVES: 4

110g (4oz) glutinous white rice
200ml (7 fl oz) thin coconut milk (optional) *with* 200ml (7 fl oz) water
or 400ml (14 fl oz) water

30g (1oz) coconut milk powder
1/2 teaspoon ground white or green cardamom
castor sugar to taste
food colouring if required
desiccated coconut

SYRUP

150ml (5 fl oz) water
100g (3½oz) castor sugar

1. Soak the rice for about 4 hours in thin coconut milk (optional) water mix, or all water.
2. Bring 225ml (9 fl oz) water to the boil.
3. Drain the rice.
4. Add the rice to the boiling water in the pan. Stir it to ensure it is not sticking to the bottom of the pan, then let it boil for about 10 to 12 minutes. It will have absorbed the water. Turn into a bowl and add the remaining ingredients apart from the syrup. Mix well, let it cool.
5. If you want to colour the balls, divide the rice mixture into the number of colours you require, plus white, and while it is still warm add a different colour to each but one batch of rice. Allow to go completely cold.
6. Meanwhile, make the syrup. Boil the water, add the sugar and boil until you get a thickish syrup.
7. Sprinkle desiccated coconut on to a work surface and roll out the mixture into balls, the size of your choice.
8. Place them in a serving bowl. Pour the syrup over the balls. Put in the fridge for 2 to 4 hours.
9. Serve chilled.

KHAO PA-SOM MAMUANG
Mango with Black and White Sticky Rice

Sweet sticky rice is one of Thailand's most popular puddings, especially when topped with sliced mango. Usually, it's white rice but I came across this combination of white and black rice at Bangkok's Royal Orchid Sheraton Hotel where they simply named it Khao Gloo-ay — orchid rice. It gets the name because of the colour the black rice gives to its boiling water. It is orchid pink. Combined with white rice, and contrasting with the orange of the mango it is quite striking, as the photograph adjacent to page 00/p8 shows. An alternative fruit to mango is star fruit.

SERVES: 4

150g (5½oz) white cooked, still warm, glutinous rice (*page 153*)

150g (5½oz) black cooked, still warm, glutinous rice (*page 152*)

30g (1oz) thick coconut milk

1 tablespoon white caster sugar

pinch of salt

2 tablespoons tinned mango juice (syrup)

4 tinned mangoes, halves

1 Cook the rices separately then mix them still warm, ensuring that enough pink water distributes evenly enough to achieve the orchid pink colour on the white rice.
2 Add the coconut sugar, salt and mango juice, mixing in well.
3 Put into a serving bowl. Top off with mango halves, sliced into strips.

KRUAY CHUEAM
Caramelized Sweet Bananas

By the time you have cooked bananas in syrup, the flavour of the actual banana is somewhat immaterial. So any bananas will do well. However, for appearance, tiny 'apple bananas', available from better greengrocers, are my favourite.

SERVES: 4

4 large or 8 apple bananas, peeled	1 cup (240ml) water
1 cup (120g/4oz) granulated sugar	½ teaspoon salt
	125ml (4 fl oz) coconut milk
	8 lemon wedges

1   Combine the sugar and water in a saucepan and simmer until it becomes a syrup – the longer you simmer the thicker the syrup – that's up to you.
2   Add the whole bananas and, keeping them whole, continue to simmer the syrup until it is thick enough to form threads off the spoon.
3   Place on to individual serving plates. Squeeze on the lemon juice and offer the coconut milk as an option, hot or cold.

KRUAY TOD
Banana Fritters

You'll find the banana fritter just about everywhere you go in the Far East. Thailand is no exception.

MAKES: 16 FRITTERS

4 large ripe bananas	1 tablespoon palm or brown sugar
1 large egg	pinch salt
2 tablespoons custard powder	milk as required
2 tablespoons cornflour or riceflour	6 tablespoons vegetable oil
2 tablespoons thick coconut milk	some castor sugar
	lime wedges

1   Mash up the banana with the egg, custard powder, flour, coconut milk, sugar and salt. You need a thick batter which drops off the spoon, so add just enough milk to achieve this.
2   Heat the oil in a flat frying pan.
3   Dollop 1 tablespoon of batter into the pan. Press it flat to make a disc about 7cm in diameter.
4   Repeat with 7 other dollops. Fry for a couple of minutes.
5   Turn over and fry the other side for a couple of minutes. If you want a perfect regular shape, you may need to shape it with a spatula as it cooks.
6   Rest on kitchen paper and repeat stages 3 to 5 for the remaining 8 fritters.
7   Dust with sugar and serve hot with lime wedges.

KHAO TOM MAT SOM
Rubies with Orange Segments

The dish with a gorgeous name, invented, of course, for the Thai royal court centuries ago. Traditionally it uses red rice water (created from black rice – see page 152).

Water chestnuts were carved into marbles (or as elaborately as the carver wished) and were steeped in the dye for 12 hours or more. Thick coconut milk cream was also dyed and just prior to serving the chestnuts were placed in the pink coconut and served. You can use cochineal to achieve this. Or you can omit it altogether and settle for white. This traditional dish is rather rich so I have modified it by incorporating raspberry yoghurt and topping off with orange segments. It tastes superb, is easy to make and it looks excellent too.

———————————— SERVES: 4 ————————————

12 tinned water chestnuts	yoghurt, raspberry flavoured
some drops of cochineal (optional)	1 tablespoon caster sugar
100g (3½oz) thick coconut milk	pinch of salt
500g (18oz) Greek-style	some orange or tangerine segments
	freshly grated coconut

1 Carve the water chestnuts to any shape you wish (or leave them as they are).
2 Add the cochineal to the water chestnut liquid from the tin.
3 Steep the water chestnuts in this liquid for 12 hours (keep it in the fridge).
4 To serve; drain the water chestnuts.
5 Mix the coconut milk and yoghurt with the sugar and salt.
6 Put it into individual serving bowls.
7 Add the water chestnuts.
8 Top off with the orange/tangerine segments (from which you have removed all pith).
9 Garnish with freshly grated coconut.
10 Serve chilled.

FUG THAWNG SANG-KHAYA
Pumpkin Custard

This is a classic Thai dish which looks harder to make than it is. A coconut custard is cooked inside a partially scooped out pumpkin. You can use a honeydew melon, alternatively. It is steamed, after which it is firm enough to cut into thin wedges. The contrast of the orange pumpkin/melon flesh against the white custard is very pretty. Its alternative name is Khanom Maw Gaeng (Baked Custard in a Melon).

SERVES: 4 OR MORE

1 20cm diameter pumpkin or honeydew melon	250ml (9 fl oz or 1 cupful) thick coconut milk
3 eggs	90g palm or brown sugar
3 egg yolks	pinch salt

1   Cut off the top of the pumpkin (or melon). Keep it aside.
2   Scoop out all the seeds leaving as much flesh as you can and creating a cavity of a size to hold about 1½ to 2 cupfuls of custard.
3   Whisk the eggs, yolks, coconut milk, sugar and salt together and pour this mixture into the pumpkin, which, depending on the cavity size, will hopefully come to the top of the hole. Put the pumpkin lid on.
4   Place the pumpkin onto a deep oven tray onto which you pour enough boiling water to come at least 6cm up the tray.
5   Put the tray into the oven, preheated to 170°C/335°F/Gas 3 1/2 and bake for 30 minutes.
6   Inspect – the custard should be nearly firm. Top up with more boiling water and bake until the custard is firm. (Actual finishing time will depend on the exact pumpkin thickness, so inspect as required.)
7   To serve, discard the top. Cut the pumpkin into wedges and serve hot or cold.

I-SA GEREEM KATEE
Coconut Ice Cream

As I've mentioned in the introduction (see page 3) elephants are very highly revered in Thailand, none more so than the so-called white elephant. In reality white elephants are pale grey or two-tone patches of dark and pale grey. They are albino, though, with pink eyes. But an elephant as white as a sheet is a mythical being – hence the expression 'a white elephant'. What's all this to do with ice cream, I hear you ask?

Ice cream is as popular in Thailand as everywhere else, although it's quite a new concept there. So new that the Thai words for ice cream are a modification of the English words. Saying 'ice cream' is as tongue twistingly hard for Thai people, as saying satay (see page 59) and the variations I have heard are '*isa-gleen*' and '*ai-tim*'.

You're still asking why elephants? Few Thais have fridges, so it's impractical for them to make ice cream at home. The ubiquitous street vendors were quick to latch on to ice cream selling, and they are supplied by factory brands. There are a number, of which my favourite is without doubt 'White Pig' brand! So all this talk about elephants, is I'm afraid a red herring. I just like talking about them!

SERVES: 4

450ml (16 fl oz) double cream	100g (3½oz) castor sugar
125ml (4 fl oz) thick coconut milk	1 teaspoon vanilla essence
	1 teaspoon custard powder
4 large eggs	pinch salt

1 Using a hand or electric whisk, mix the eggs, sugar, vanilla, custard powder and salt together.

2 Heat the cream and coconut milk in a non-stick pan, stirring frequently, until it starts simmering.

3 Then transfer it to a large heat-proof glass bowl which fits comfortably over a saucepan of boiling water.

4 Once the milk is simmering, whisk in the egg mixture. Keep whisking until the mixture is thick enough to coat a spoon.

5 Allow it to cool. Transfer to suitable tub(s). Place in the freezer for about 3 hours. Remove and mix thoroughly. This breaks down ice crystals.

6 Repeat an hour later. Do this 2 or 3 times – the more you do it, the smoother the ice cream – then leave it to freeze properly (24 hours minimum) until you wish to use it.

7   Allow it about 10 minutes to soften a little before serving. Dip your
ice cream scoop into warm water between each scoop.

NOTE: *If you have an ice cream maker, churn it according to its instructions until
you get the required texture, and serve.*

VARIATION

I-SA GEREEN KATEE MANUANG
Mango Ice Cream

A delicious variation is to add pulped mango to the above ice cream recipe.

────────────────── SERVES: 4 ──────────────────

2 halves tinned Alphonso sweet mangoes

1   Pulp the mango halves down to a purée.
2   Stir the purée into the ice cream mixture at the end of stage 4 above.
3   Proceed to the end of that recipe.

LEMON GRASS TEA

Here is a totally refreshing brew. It is designed to be enjoyed boiling hot, of
course, but for an exciting change, chill it, add crushed ice and sip it on
the hottest summer day! Apparently it was a favourite 'tipple' of Queen
Victoria. We are amused!

────────────────── PER CUP ──────────────────

1 stalk lemon grass, cut tassel method (*page 30*)
1 teaspoon honey (optional)
squeeze of fresh lime juice

1   Boil 200ml (7 fl oz) water in a pan with the lemon grass.
2   Transfer to a cup. Add the honey and lemon.

FACING PAGE   Foreground: Red Curry with Fish (page 141); behind: Seafood Salad (page 83), and in the tiny bowl, Chilli Jam (page 170).

FACING NEXT PAGE   Sugared Toasted Cashews (page 182), Mangoes with Black and White Sticky Rice (page 184) and Rubies with Orange Segments (page 186).

APPENDIX 1

THE CURRY CLUB

PAT CHAPMAN always had a deep-rooted interest in spicy food, curry in particular, and over the years he built up a huge pool of information which he felt could be usefully passed on to others. He conceived the idea of forming an organization for this purpose.

Since it was founded in January, 1982, The Curry Club has built up a membership of several thousands. We have a marchioness, some lords and ladies, knights a-plenty, a captain of industry or two, generals, admirals and air marshals (not to mention a sprinkling of ex-colonels), and we have celebrities – actresses, politicians, rock stars and sportsmen. We have an airline, a former Royal Navy warship, and a hotel chain.

We have fifteen members whose name is Curry or Curries, twenty called Rice and several with the name Spice or Spicier, Cook, Fry, Frier or Fryer and one Boiling. We have a Puri (a restaurant owner), a Paratha and a Nan and a good many Mills and Millers, one Dal and a Lentil, an Oiler, a Gee (but no Ghee), and a Butter but no Marji (several Marjories though, and a Marjoram and a Minty). We also have several Longs and Shorts, Thins and Broads, one Fatt and one Wide, and a Chilley and a Coole.

We have members on every continent including a good number of Asian members, but by and large the membership is a typical cross-section of the Great British Public, ranging in age from teenage to dotage, and in occupation from refuse collectors to receivers, high street traders to high court judges, tax inspectors to taxi drivers. There are students and pensioners, millionaires and unemployed... thousands of people who have just one thing in common – a love of curry and spicy foods.

Members receive a bright and colourful quarterly magazine, which has regular features on curry and the curry lands. It includes news items, recipes, reports on restaurants, picture features, and contributions from members and professionals alike. The information is largely concerned with curry, but by popular demand it now includes regular input on other exotic and spicy cuisines such as those of Thailand, the spicy Americas, the Middle East and China. We produce a wide selection of publications, including the books listed on page ii.

Obtaining some of the ingredients required for curry cooking can be difficult, but The Curry Club makes it easy, with a comprehensive range of products, including spice mixes, chutneys, pickles, papadoms, sauces and curry pastes. These are available from major food stores and specialist delicatessens up and down the country. If they are not stocked near you, there is the Club's well-established and efficient mail-order service. Hundreds of items are stocked, including spices, pickles, pastes, dry foods, tinned foods, gift items, publications and specialist kitchen and tableware.

On the social side, the Club holds residential weekend cookery courses and gourmet nights at selected restaurants. Top of the list is our regular Curry Club gourmet trip to India and other spicy countries. We take a small group of curry enthusiasts to the chosen country and tour the incredible sights, in between sampling the delicious food of each region.

If you would like more information about The Curry Club, write (enclosing a stamped addressed envelope, please) to: The Curry Club, PO Box 7, Haslemere, Surrey, GU27 1EP.

GALANGAL

APPENDIX 2

THE STORE CUPBOARD

THE ITEMS listed include the spices and specialist non-perishable ingredients needed to make the recipes in this book. I have not given quantities because they vary from manufacturer to manufacturer. The items marked * are used in many of the recipes. The others are frequently called for.

Many items listed are available by post from The Curry Club, see Appendix 1. Supermarkets, such as Sainsbury, also have good ranges of specialist ingredients.

Sugar
* palm sugar (*nam taa peep*)
brown sugar
castor sugar
granulated sugar
white rock sugar

Tinned
baby sweetcorn
beansprouts
black or yellow soya beans
bamboo shoots
water chestnuts
straw mushrooms
mangoes in syrup

Various
clear honey
cloud ear (dried) mushrooms
peanut butter
shelled raw peanuts
shelled raw cashew nuts
* shrimp paste (*kapee*)
* dried prawns

rice flour
rice vinegar
rice wine
sea salt
tamarind block
tomato chutney
tomato purée
wine vinegar

Sauces
light soy sauce
dark soy sauce
sweet soy sauce
    (ketchup manis)
oyster sauce
* fish sauce

Dried Noodles
egg noodles (*ba-mee*)
flat rice noodles (*sen-lek*)
glass noodles (*num-sen*)
wiry rice noodles (*sen-mee*)
vermicelli noodles
    (*kuaytiaw jeen*)

Coconut
  coconut desiccated
  * coconut milk tinned
  * coconut milk powder

Oils
  * sunflower
  * soya
  vegetable
  sesame

Rice
  * jasmine and/or basmati, long
    grained rice
  Thai black glutinous rice
  Thai white glutinous rice

Spices – ground
  chilli
  * coriander

* cummin
paprika
* turmeric
* white pepper

Spices – whole
  bay leaves
  black peppercorns
  cassia bark
  cloves
  coriander seed
  cummin seeds
  dried bird's eye chillies
  * green peppercorns dried
    and/or in brine
  * lime leaves, dried
  star aniseed
  white or green cardamom
  white sesame seed

Bottled Items
These should only be bought as substitutes for fresh items. Blue Dragon Thai range is available worldwide.

minced basil
minced chilli
minced coriander
minced garlic

minced ginger
lemon grass sticks in water
green curry paste
red curry paste

THAI GLOSSARY

THIS EXTENSIVE glossary includes some items not specifically mentioned in the recipes. It is intended to be used as a general reference work. It is also worth checking the index to see whether a particular word you want can be found elsewhere.

As certain Thai ingredients are used in the food of neighbouring countries, I have in relevant cases given Burmese, Malayan, Indonesian, Philipino, Laoation and Vietnamese words too, in order to help you locate the ingredients at specialist stores.

A
aahaan – food
aahaan pa – jungle food
aubergine – *makua muang*
    pea – *makua puong*

B
baan – house
bai – leaf
bai kari – curry leaf
bai kruay – banana leaf
bai toey – screwpine leaf
    (pandanus)
bamboo – *phai*
bamboo shoot – *normai*
banana – *kruay*
basil – (see p28)
    sweet basil – *horapa*
    bai manglak – bush basil
    bai grapao or *krapa* – holy
    basil

bai makroot – lime leaf
bai krawan – cassia leaf
bai saranae – mint leaf
Bangkok – *krung thep*
    (City of Angels)
bay leaf – see cassia leaf
bean – *tua*

bean curd – *taohou*
    fried – *tao nagork tod*
    pickled – *tao nagork yee*
    sprout – *tua nagork*
beef – *nua* or *neau*
bergamot – see lime leaves
bread – *kanom pan*
breeo – sour
breeo wan – sweet and sour
bua luang – lotus

C
cabbage – *galum plee/galumbee*
cashew nut
cardamom – *luk gravan*
cassia – *ob cheuy*
cassia leaves – *bai krawan*
cauliflower – *dauk ka lam*
ceun chai – celery
chaa – tea
cheen – Chinese
cheh – soak
chicken – *gai*
chilli – *prig* – see also *prig*
chilli – There are a great many
    varieties of chilli, which are the
    fleshy pods of shrub-like bushes
    of the capsicum family. Chillies
    range from large to small, and

colours include green, white, purple, pink and red. They are now the most important heat agent in Thai cookery. They vary in hotness from mild to incendiary-like potency. (see p32)

chilli powder – *prig pon*

Chinese – *Cheen* or *jiin*

chud/jued/jeud – clear soup/ consommé, minimally spiced

cinnamon – *ob cheuy*

clove – *gram poo* or *kran ploo*

coconut – *maprao*

coconut milk – *nam katee*

Cooking terms

  boil – *tom*

  bake – *ob*

  bake/toast/roast – *bing*

  raw/half cooked – *dip*

  boil/cook in water – *dom/tom*

  deep-fry – *tod/tord*

  fried – *hor*

  fry – *haeng*

  soak – *cheh*

  steam – *nueng/doon*

  stir-fry – *pad*

  fried – *dao*

  pound/pulverize – *dum*

  refrigerator – *too yen*

Cooking utensils

  cherng kran – cooking (portable) stove

  kude maprao – coconut grater

  krok/sok – mortar/pestle

  ka po – perforated press mould

  krathong – shell shaped brass mould to make batter cups

coriander leaf – *pak chee*

coriander seed – *look pak chee* or *mellet pak chee*

crab – *poo/bu*

cucumber – *taeng kwa*

cummin – *mellet yira (yeera)*

curry – *karee* – is only used to describe Indian-style curries in Thailand, and they are different from Thai curries (see *khaeng*)

  green curry – *khaeng keo wan*

  hot Thai curry – *khaeng ped* (*khaeng* is liquid *ped* is peppery)

  mild curry – *khaeng karee*

  Moslem curry – *khaeng mat saman* or *Mussaman*

  see also *krung* (paste)

curry pastes – *krung*

  red curry paste – *krung khaeng ped daeng* – mainly for meat (beef)

  green curry paste – *krung khaeng keo wan* – mainly poultry

  orange curry paste – *krung khaeng som* – often shrimp/prawn

  yellow curry paste – *krung khaeng leung* – mainly chicken/beef

  Mussaman krung khaeng – in Moslem style

  Panaeng krung khaeng – in Malay style

D

Danu keson – type of mint used in soups (Malay, Thai, Vietnamese)

dauk chand – mace

dauk ka lam – cauliflower

daun pandan – long pointed pandanus (screwpine) leaf used to flavour curry (Malay, Thai, Vietnamese) and wrap around food parcels

deep-fry – *tod*

dessert – *khong wan*

dom – boil

dong – pickle

dried fish – *pla haeng*

dried shrimp – *gung haeng*

dry – *haeng*
duck – *ped*

E
egg – *kai*
    hard-boiled – *kai tom*
    fried – *kai dao*
    scrambled – *kai kuan*
    omelette – *kai jiaw/jiew*
eggplant – see aubergine

F
fish types
    cat fish – *pla duk*
    cockles/clam – *hoi lai*
    crab – *poo*
    cuttlefish – *pla nueg*
    eel – *pla lai*
    grouper – *pla phad*
    lobster – *gung ta lay*
    mackerel – *pla in see*
    mussel – *hoy man poo*
    oyster – *hoy harng rom*
    pomfret – *pla chalamet*
    prawn – *gung foi*
    scallop – *hoy phat*
    sea bass – *pla ka pong*
    shark – *pla chalarm*
    shark fin – *hoo pla chalarm*
    shrimp – *gung narng*
    squid – *pla muek*
    tuna – *pla o*
fish – *pla*
fish sauce – *nam pla* (Thai)
    nga pya (Burmese)
    nvoc nan (Vietnamese)
    patis (Philippine)
    It is the runny liquid strained from fermented anchovies, and is a very important flavouring agent.
frog (leg) – *gohp/kob*
fruit types
    durian – durian
    kanoon – jackfruit

lamut – sapodilla
lan yai – longan
leenchee – lychee
mafueng – star apple, carambola
malakor – papaya
mamuang – mango
mungkut – mangosteen
noi nar – custard apple
puak – taro
sakay – breadfruit
supparot – pineapple

G
gaeng – soup/spicy broth/curry – *see khaeng*
gaeng chud – consommé (bland not spicy)
gai – chicken
galangal –
    A tuber related to ginger which comes in varieties called greater or lesser. It has a more peppery taste than ginger (which can be substituted for it). It is used in Thai cooking where it is called *kha*, and in Indonesia *(laos)* and Malay *(kenkur)*. It is available in the UK in fresh form (rare), dried or powdered.
greater galangal – creamy flesh, delicate flavour, used extensively.
    kha (Thai)
    Lengkuas (Indonesia)
    Laos (Indonesian)
lesser galangal
alpinia galanga
(or lesser ginger) – or *Zeodary*.
    Orange-red flesh, less delicate.
    krachai (Thai)
    kencur (Malay)
    Can be powdered – (*kaempferia Pandurata*)
galumbee/galum plee – cabbage
garlic – *kratiam*
ginger – *khing kha tue*

197

ginger, lesser – *krachai* (galangal)
gohp/kob – frogs' legs
gram poo – clove
grat dook – meat chop/spare rib
grob – crispy
gueuteow – see noodles (all types)
gun chian – dried pork sausage
gung – prawns/lobster
    (crustaceans)
gung foi – prawns
gung narng – small prawns
gung ta lay – lobster

H
haeng – dry
haeo cheen – water chestnut
hed – mushroom
hed hom – dried chinese mushroom
hor – fried
hor mok – steamed curry served in
    banana leaf
horapa – *see* basil
hua hom – onion

J
jasmine essence – *yod nam*
jasmine – *malee* – used in desserts and
    rice
jeow/jiaw – fried
jiin – Chinese – see cheen
KK
kaffir – lime leaves
kai – egg
kai jiaw – omelette
kanom – cake
kanom pan – bread
kaopot – sweetcorn
kapee – *see* shrimp paste
karee – curry
kencur powder – *see galingal*
khem – salty
kha – *see galangal*
kha min – turmeric root
khaeng – curry liquid or spicy soup

khao – *see* rice
khao niaw – glutinous rice
khao pad – fried rice
khantoke – north-eastern style of for-
    mal eating (banquet), seating at
    low tables
khing – ginger
khong wan – dessert (sweet food)
klong – river or canal
klong krang – board to make shells
krachai – lesser ginger
krachup – water chestnut
krapal – *see* basil
kratiam – garlic
kratong – banana leaf cup
kratong mould makes batter cups
krob (see grob) – crispy
kruay – banana
krung – paste
krung khaeng – *see* curry paste
kuaytiaw – noodle
kude maprao – coconut grater
kung – *see gung*

L
lao – liquor
laap – *issan* – kind of steak tartare
lemon grass – *takrai* (Thai)
    serai (Malay)
    A fragrant leafed plant which
    imparts a subtle lemony
    flavour to cooking. Use
    ground powder (made from
    the bulb) as a substitute.
lettuce – *pak kaat*
lime – *manau*
lime leaves – *makrut* or citrus leaves.
    Used, fresh or dried to give a
    distinctive aromatic flavour.
    kaffir (Indonesian)
    powdered/ground – *pew*
    makrut
lobster – *gung ta lay*
look chand – nutmeg

look gravan – cardamom
look pak chee – coriander seed
lon – sauces cooked with chilli and
    coconut milk

M

mace – *dauk chand*
ma la kor – papaya
mai – bamboo shoot
makrut/makroot – *see* lime leaves
mak kam – tamarind
makua – aubergine
makua puong – pea aubergine
makua taet – tomato
mangluk (bai) – sweet basil (leaf)
mamuang – mango
man – balls (meat balls)
man – yam
man farang – potato
man thet – sweet potato
manao – lime
mango – *mamuang*
maprao – coconut
meat – *neua/nua*
    beef – *nua*
    lamb – *kaeh* or *nua look gaa*
    moo – pork
    nua – beef
    pork – *moo*
mellet pak chee – coriander seeds
mellet yira – caraway, cummin,
    fennel
milk – *nom*
mint – *see danu keson* and *bai saranae*
moo – pork
mortar and pestle – *krok* and *sak*
mushroom – *hed*
    straw mushroom – *hed faang*
    dried Chinese cloud-ear – *hed hoo
    nu*
    oyster
    dried – *hed haeng*

N

nam – water
nam cha – tea
nam katee – coconut milk
nam man – oil
nam man hoi – oyster sauce
nam pla – *see* fish sauce
nam prig – chilli sauce
nam som – sour water (vinegar,
    orange)
nam tan – sugar/syrup
nam tan peep or puek – palm sugar
nem – spicy sausage
neua – meat
nom – milk
noodle – *kuaytiaw* See also p157
normai – bamboo shoot
nua – beef
nueng – steam
nut – *tua*
nutmeg – *loo chand*

O

ob – bake (*op*)
ob cheuy – cinnamon/cassia
oi – sugar cane
okra – *kra jeap*
omelette – *kai jiaw*
onion – *hua hom*
orange – *som*
oyster sauce – *nam man hoy*

P

pa – jungle
paad – mince
pad – stir-fry
pak – vegetables, green leafed
pak chee farang – parsley
pak chee – coriander leaf
pak kaat – lettuce
pak kaat hau – white radish
pak thawng – pumpkin
pandanahs leaf – *bai toey*
panaeng – peanut based (Malaysian)
    curry sauce

papaya – *ma la kor*
parsley – *pak chee farang*
pasin – sarong like, traditional long skirt
paste – *krung* (curry paste)
paw pia – spring rolls
pea aubergine – *makua puong*
peanut – *tua lisong, sei pancreng*
ped – duck
pew makrut – ground lime leaf
phet – pungent, peppery, spicy
pickle – *dong*
pineapple – *supparot*
ping – skewer
pla – fish
pla grob – smoked fish
pla kem – salted (dried) fish
pla raa – fermented fish
poo – crab
pork – *moo*
poultry
    bird – *nok*
    chicken – *gai*
    duck – *ped*
    quail – *nok kra ta*
poy kak bua – star aniseed
praew – sour – *see also breeo*
prawn family (crustaceans) – *gung*
prawns – *gung foi*
prig – chilli
prig chee – long red chilli
prig haeng – dried chilli
prig pon – chilli powder
prig thai – black pepper
prig toom – bell pepper
puak – *taro/dasheen*
pumpkin – *pak thawng (fug thong)*
pungent – *phet*

Q
quail – *nok kra-ta*

R
raa – *see pla raa*
radish white – *pak kaat hua*
ram wong – Thai dance circle

rempah – *see daun pandan* (Malay)
rice – *khao*
    khao haun malee – jasmine fragrant rice
    khao jao – ordinary rice
    khao niaw – sticky (glutinous) rice
rice noodles – *see noodle*

S
sago – *saku*
salad – *yam*
salt – *kem* or *kua* or *glua* (rock salt *kem med*)
saus prig (bottled) – chilli sauce
sausage (dried pork) – *gun chiang*
sen lek – wiry rice noodle
sen mee – small rice noodle
sen yai – rice stick noodle
sesame seed (white) – *tee olaa*
sesame seed (black) – *nga*
shrimp paste – *kapi*
    Usually in rectangular block, dark brown in colour or greyish yellow.
    blachan (Malayan)
    nga pi (Burmese)
    kapi (Thai).
    mam tom (Vietnam)
    Vital flavouring for the cooking of those countries.
shrimps – *see* prawns
    gung narng
    – *see* fish
sii yu – soy sauce
soak – *cheh*
som – orange
som or pomello, shaddock, Thai grapefruit, *shatkora*
sord sai – stuffed
soy sauce – *nam siiyu*
soy bean – *tua lueang*
sweet – *wan*
sweet and sour – *breeo wan*
sweetcorn – *kaopot*
spicy – *ped*
spring onions – *ton hom*

spring roll – *paw pia*
star aniseed – *poy kak bua*
steam – *nueng*
stuffed – *sod sai* or *yad sai*
sugar – *nam tan (tal)*
sugar cane – *oi*
supparot – pineapple

T
taeng kwa – cucumber
taeng mo – watermelon
takrai – *see* lemon grass
talay – seafood
tamarind – *mak kam*
taro – *puak*
tao hou – bean curd
At table
    fork – *sawm*
    spoon – *chawn*
    chopsticks – *ta kiap*
    recipe – *dam rap*
    restaurant – *raan aharn*
    menu – *ma noo*
    glass – *kaew*
tee ola – sesame seed
tod – deep-fried
tofu – *see* bean curd
tom – boil
tomato – *makua taet*
tong – bag, basket, cup – *see kratong*
ton hom – spring onions
tua – bean or nut
tua fak yaw – long bean
tua nagork – beansprout
turmeric – *kha min*

U
uon – fat, plump

V
vegetables – *pak mangsawirat*
    asparagus – *naw mai farang*
    aubergine – *makua*
    banana flower – *hua plee*
    bean – *tua*

    beansprout – *tua nagork*
    cabbage (white) – *galum plee*
    celery – *kuen chai*
    bitter gourd – *mara*
    bottle gourd – *nam tao*
    cucumber – *taeng kwa*
    long bean – *tua fak yaw*
    melon – *fug*
    mushroom – *hed*
    okra – *kra jeap (jiab)*
    onion – *hua hom*
    pepper (green bell) – *prik toom*
    pumpkin – *fug thong*
    ribbed gourd – *buab*
    spinach – *pak boong*
    spiny gourd (kakrol) – *pak khaao*
    sweetcorn – *kao pot*
    tamarind – *makaam*
    taro – *puak*
    tomato – *makua taet*
    white radish – *pak kaat hua*
vermicelli noodle – *wun sen*

W
wan – sweet
water – *nam*
watermelon – *taeng mo*
water chestnut – *krachup* or *haco cheen*
wun sen – vermicelli noodle

Y
yaang – BBQ, roasted, grill
ya dong – herbal liquor
yai – large
yam – salad, often with meat or seafood (pronounced 'yum')
yam – (potato-like tuber) – *man*
yeera – cummin – *see mellet yira*
yen – cold
yum – salad

INDEX